For digital entrepreneurs

THE
SOCIAL
COMMERCE
HANDBOOK

20 SECRETS FOR TURNING SOCIAL MEDIA INTO SOCIAL SALES

PAUL MARSDEN
PAUL CHANEY

New York   Chicago   San Francisco   Lisbon   London
Madrid   Mexico City   Milan   New Delhi   San Juan
Seoul   Singapore   Sydney   Toronto

Sections of this book were originally published in *The F-Commerce Handbook* (McGraw-Hill, 2012) by the same authors of this book.

1 2 3 4 5 6 7 8 9 10   DOC/DOC   1 8 7 6 5 4 3 2

ISBN   978-0-07-180202-4
MHID   0-07-180202-9

e-ISBN 978-0-07-180203-1
e-MHID   0-07-180203-7

McGraw-Hill books are available at special quantity discounts to use as premiums and sales promotions or for use in corporate training programs. To contact a representative, please e-mail us at bulksales@mcgraw-hill.com.

This book is printed on acid-free paper.

CONTENTS

Introduction

It's all about the money, the rest is just conversation.

—GORDON GEKKO, *WALL STREET*

"How do I sell with social media?" It's a deceptively simple question, and one that an increasing number of businesses, brands and entrepreneurs are asking today. It's also a question that we chose to dodge during one of our social media workshops back in 2010. Our evasive reply was that it was the wrong question—social media was not about selling, it was about connecting, collaborating, and communicating more effectively.

Two years and one blog—*Social Commerce Today*—later, we're now ready to answer the question properly. *The Social Commerce Handbook* is our answer to the question of how to sell with social media. It is a practical handbook for businesses and entrepreneurs looking to turn social media into social sales. In 20 bite-size chapters, we'll reveal 20 secrets to unlocking sales with social media from pioneers in the new field of social commerce; selling with social media.

SHOW ME THE MONEY!

If you've picked up this book, you probably already "get" social media. You realize that social media, online media that supports social interaction and user contributions[1] is big media; one in nine humans use YouTube every month and more, one in seven, use Facebook. So you "get" that social media is emerging as an important media channel for reaching and interacting with your customers and prospects. Whether they're busy polishing their résumés on LinkedIn, sharing business smarts and ideas on Quora, sharing content on Instagram, Pinterest, or YouTube, or sharing their lives on Facebook, social media is where you'll increasingly find your customers.

And if you "get" social media, you see beyond the hype and spin of social media zealots and realize that social media is *not* a revolution. It's just media—with its own peculiar advantages and disadvantages. It's fast, relatively scalable, interactive, and supports multimedia content. But it's also uncontrolled, uncontrollable, and largely unproven as an effective medium for advertising. Nevertheless, as a medium for word of mouth, social media is incredibly effective, and as a business you'll know that word of mouth matters. We live in a recommendation economy where reputation is everything, and reputation is not built on what you say about yourself, but what other people say about you.

For example, a recent cross-industry analysis by the consulting firm Bain found that the most recommended business in any competitive set grows far faster (two and half times as fast, on average) than its competitors.[2] Which is why, of course, the simple question, "How likely is it that you'd recommend us?" has been dubbed the Ultimate Question in business. Increase word of mouth by just 12 percent, and you'll double your growth, says Bain. For instance, Apple figures that for every $1 an Apple fan spends on its products, that fan brings in a further $.79 of business through word-of-mouth recommendations.[3]

Social media has commercial value for your business because social media unleashes word of mouth, allowing more people to recommend more, more easily, and to more people. Put simply, social media matters to your business because it is word of mouth on steroids.

So, while you may "get" social media and why it matters, you may not yet "get" how to make social media pay. Sure, you can treat social media like traditional media and sink advertising money into it. Or you can spend money, time, and resources on social media by using it as an online channel for customer service or relationship marketing. But how do you make money, rather than spend money on social media? Social commerce offers a simple answer: Use social media as a smart sales channel and you'll sell better, faster, and more efficiently than ever before. That's the promise of social commerce.

WHAT IS SOCIAL COMMERCE ANYWAY? FROM MOLIÈRE TO MADE.COM

So what exactly is "social commerce"? In short, social commerce is selling with social media, online media that supports social interaction and user contributions. It's selling with the current "Big Five"—YouTube, Pinterest, Twitter, Facebook, and LinkedIn, as well as through other social media platforms such as Quora, Instagram, and Google+.

Interestingly, however, the term "social commerce" itself was first used in a literary critique of the seventeenth-century French playwright Molière.[4] Here, social commerce described "social transactions" in which reputations and public "social" images were exchanged instead of money. Sports brand Nike has recently revived this idea with an innovative custom Facebook application that allows people to bid for and buy Nike sneakers with their reputation rather than money—in the form of points earned through Nike+ applications.[5] Social commerce is about using social media as "transactional media" to complete sales transactions, but in some of the most innovative cases of social commerce, no money changes hands.

Since becoming popular in 2005, the term social commerce has evolved to mean any kind of commerce that uses "user content" to sell. So social commerce can range from e-commerce on social media sites, to social media features on e-commerce sites. And through mobile devices, social commerce is venturing into traditional brick-and-mortar commerce, allowing people to connect, collaborate, and even transact together when they shop in store.

Industry thought-leader Steve Rubel from the PR firm Edelman sums up the umbrella term of social commerce nicely: social commerce is about "creating places where people can collaborate online, get advice from trusted individuals, find goods and services, and then purchase them."[6] And while there are many ways to skin this social commerce cat, four distinct areas of social commerce have evolved.

- **Social Applications for E-Commerce Sites** that enable vendors to collect and share user feedback—ratings, reviews, and recommendations—on their site and through their customers' social networks, and personalize the e-commerce experience. These apps range from simple social sharing plug-ins that add sharing buttons such as the Pinterest "Pin" button to product pages, to social plug-ins that add Amazon-style ratings and reviews features to an e-commerce site. These apps not only accelerate and amplify the word of mouth, but can also allow vendors to predict demand and offer personalized recommendations based on similarities between shopper profiles ("people who liked that, liked this"-style technology).

- **E-Commerce Applications for Social Sites** that help vendors sell directly in social media such as from their blog, YouTube channel, or Facebook Page. These range from simple storefront plug-ins that republish an external e-commerce site on a social media page to standalone e-commerce applications for social media. E-commerce apps for social media sites have been particularly popular with small and medium-size businesses, providing a cost-effective and simple alternative to maintaining a traditional e-commerce site. Market leader Payvment currently has over 150,000 businesses using its social media e-commerce application.
- **Mobile Applications for In-store Social Shopping** that help people shop smarter by shopping together via mobile handsets. These range from mobile apps for "group-buying," which allow people to get store discounts by clubbing together and buying in bulk, to mobile apps that help store visitors get instant feedback from their friends on whether or what to buy. Mobile apps for in-store social shopping also include so-called "check-in" apps such as foursquare, which reward people for sharing where they are shopping, as well as a new generation of mobile "ACT" apps (Assistive Consumer Technology), which add a social "augmented reality" layer to the store experience, displaying shared reviews, ratings, and recommendations when the handset is pointed at particular products.
- **Web Applications for Social Shopping** that enable vendors to promote and sell their products on sites where shoppers congregate, share, exchange, and buy. These range from shopping club sites such as Fab and Gilt that run regular retail events for vendors, to community-based marketplaces such as Etsy and Shoply, which allow vendors to cultivate one-to-one relationships with their customers. Web apps for social shopping also include platforms such as The Fancy, Svpply, and Pinterest,

SOCIAL APPS FOR E-COMMERCE	E-COMMERCE APPS FOR SOCIAL SITES
MOBILE APPS FOR SOCIAL SHOPPING	WEB APPS FOR SOCIAL SHOPPING

The Four Areas of Social Commerce

which offer aggregated and curated product selections—as well as sites such as Made.com, which allow designers to submit product designs, which if popular, go into production.

Throughout *The Social Commerce Handbook* you'll discover secrets to unlocking sales in each of these four areas of social commerce. However, rather than organize the handbook around each of these areas, we've opted for an insight-led approach. What we've learned from two years of social commerce research is that if an insight is useful in one area of social commerce, it's also usually useful and applicable in another. And because technology and applications change and evolve so fast, they are not the place for a book. That's what the Internet is for. So a word of warning, if you are looking for a guide to select or deploy this or that social commerce application or technology—this is not where you'll find it. Instead, *The Social Commerce Handbook* is designed to provide you with a set of insight-led guiding principles to help you unlock the sales potential of social media today and tomorrow—whatever the technology deployed. We've looked at what's working and what isn't and used insights from sales psychology and social psychology to explain it, most notably drawing on the work of Dr. Robert Cialdini,[7] a specialist in both fields. If you are familiar with Cialdini's research, you'll see that we are greatly indebted to his work.

SAY HELLO TO THE SOLOMO SHOPPER

Although the 20 secrets revealed in *The Social Commerce Handbook* are diverse and eclectic, two major themes emerge when they are viewed together. The first is that social commerce tends to work best when you are selling to a new breed of consumer—the "SOLOMO consumer," i.e., people who shop smart with SOcial, LOcation-aware and MObile technology. Consider the following:[8]

Social:
- 23 percent: Online time people spend with social media—social networking is now the #1 online activity
- 86 percent: People who consult online reviews before buying; 90 percent trust the reviews they read
- 42 percent: Proportion of U.S. online adults who follow a retailer via Facebook, Twitter, or blog
- 6: The average number of brands or businesses people follow in social media
- 56 percent: Facebook users who have clicked through to a retailer website from a Facebook post
- 28 percent: Facebook users who have purchased something online via a link on Facebook
- 35 percent: People who would buy products on Facebook; 32 percent would do so from Twitter, if possible

- 25 percent: Google searches done on the YouTube video sharing site; YouTube is the world's second largest search engine
- 52 percent: People who share deals from local deal sites such as Groupon and LivingSocial
- 50 percent+: People more likely to buy from businesses they follow in social media
- 53 percent: People on Twitter who recommend companies and/or products in their Tweets
- 12x: Degree of trust people have in shared consumers reviews compared to business-communicated information
- 90 percent: People trusting recommendations from people they know; 70 percent trust opinions of unknown users

Local:
- 300 percent: User growth of location-based services in 2010— services that have evolved from games to include reviews, recommendations, and deals
- 95 percent: Mobile users using their mobile devices to find local information; 88 percent take action based on that information
- 70 percent: Online mobile users who use their mobile devices to help shopping in-store
- 47 percent: People who access customer reviews in-store via mobile devices
- 86 percent: People using the web to find local businesses: 20 percent+ of all Google searches have a local intent
- 78 percent: Mobile users who have purchased from a local deals site
- 76 percent: Smartphone owners who have made an in-store purchase based on information accessed from their phone
- 49 percent: Smartphone users who use their phones to get local promotions and coupons
- 45 percent: Online European consumers who have researched a product online and then bought it in a shop

- $61 billion: Projected value of the online local deals market in 2015; up 138 percent from 2011

Mobile:
- 7.5 percent: Total media consumption on a mobile device
- 16 percent: Google searches made on a mobile device, up 400 percent in last 12 months
- 63 percent: Smartphone users who use their phone to access social networks at least once a week
- 79 percent: Smartphone users using their mobile devices to help with shopping
- 35 percent: Smartphone owners who have made a purchase with their phones
- 34 percent: Facebook users accessing Facebook from mobile devices at least once a day (32 percent view YouTube videos on a daily basis from a mobile device)
- 32 percent: People using mobile devices to browse or research products or services at least once a month
- 2015: The year web access from mobile devices will overtake desktop access
- 15 percent: People completing transactions with their mobile devices at least once a month

We believe SOLOMO technology is creating a perfect storm in commerce, causing a disruptive paradigm shift in how to sell successfully. Whether it's shopping for business services or consumer products, people are adopting SOLOMO technology—social, location-aware, and mobile—to help them research, choose, and buy smarter. So the first big secret of social commerce is to think outside the social box when selling with social media. Think social, local, and mobile and sell to the new SOLOMO customer with real-time, on-demand, and on-the-go value.

SOCIAL UTILITY

The second big theme that emerges in *The Social Commerce Handbook* is that social commerce success usually means selling with *social utility*—being socially useful to customers by helping them shop smart with their social intelligence, and by offering them social status or social bonding opportunities. This may sound like psychobabble, but we think social utility—helping customers solve problems socially and helping them solve their social problems—is proving to be critical to social commerce success.

> **Solving Problems Socially**—offering people the means to use their "social intelligence," their ability to understand and learn from each other and profit from social situations when they shop. This might include tools to help people discover, evaluate, and decide socially based on shared experience. Or it might include tools to help people profit socially, that is, through cooperation or collective action, such as clubbing together to get bulk discounts.
>
> **Solving Social Problems**—helping people find solutions to their social goals, such as looking good in the eyes of others through, for example, some privileged access to a new product. Without getting bogged down in social psychology, social problems often boil down to one of two kinds: problems of *social bonding* and problems of *social status*. Social bonding is all about doing things for others in order to deepen social relationships and to "fit in" with others. Social status, on the other hand, is about the opposite. It is about differentiating ourselves to "stand out" by projecting a social image based on being different and better. Social commerce works when you're selling solutions to these two core social problems as well as your product or service.

If the *The Social Commerce Handbook* has one key message or insight, it is that social utility is the central and sustainable value proposition of social commerce, and the true secret for turning social media into social sales. *The big secret to selling with social media is to offer social utility by deploying social technology that helps people solve problems socially and solve social problems.* This involves adopting a "social mindset" when thinking about commerce in social media—understanding why people use social media (for social bonding, social status, and social intelligence), and developing a value proposition that delivers on these contextual needs. This social mindset then needs to be combined with a more traditional "commercial mindset"; to sell successfully in social media (or elsewhere) you'll need to deliver on a differentiated and compelling value proposition that is genuinely unique. Like two curved pillars of an arch, a social mindset and a commerce mindset support each other in social commerce. Without one, the other collapses—and where social commerce has failed it is usually because one of the mindsets is missing.

THE 20 SECRETS REVEALED

Primed with a new social commerce mindset and armed with the concepts of the SOLOMO consumer and social utility, how do you actually go about selling with social media? For a full answer, including insights and practical recommendations, you'll of course need to read the book. But here, as a brief summary, are the 20 secrets for turning social media into social sales:

1. **Play the Impulse Game:** The secret to unlocking sales with social media is to sell impulse products—unplanned purchases that offer instant gratification and make people either feel good, look good, or get good value.

2. **Involve Them:** The secret to unlocking sales with social media is to involve your customers as advisors or contributors with simple, easy, one-click "add-an-egg" social media initiatives.

3. **The Experiential Imperative:** The secret to unlocking sales with social media is to use social media to run online experiential retail events worth talking about.

4. **Incentivize Intelligently:** The secret to unlocking sales with social media is to offer social incentives that reward people for shopping together.

5. **Sell with Scarcity:** The secret to unlocking sales with social media is to offer your customers enhanced social status with social media limited editions and early access to new products.

6. **Build Consistency:** The secret to unlocking sales with social media is through progressive and public upselling that takes customers from "Like" to "Loyalty."

7. **Reciprocity Rules:** The secret to unlocking sales with social media is gifting, either offering free samples yourself, or encouraging gifting between customers.

8. **Social Validation:** The secret to unlocking sales with social media is sell with "social proof," allowing customers to shop smart with their social intelligence by learning from the shared experiences of others.

9. **Arm Yourself with Authority:** The secret to unlocking sales with social media is to use the voice of borrowed authority when selling: expert picks, endorsements, and testimonials.

10. **Like and Be Loved:** The secret to unlocking sales with social media is to sell through affinity networks, helping friends help their friends with your products and services.

11. **Drive Discovery:** The secret to unlocking sales with social media is to drive product discovery through a fusion of the "social graph" and the "interest graph"—where personal connections meet shared interests.

12. **Be Purpose-Driven:** The secret to unlocking sales with social media is to start with a purpose and be people-focused not

product-focused. Stand for something and your customers will stand together for you.

13. **Deliver ZMOTS:** The secret to unlocking sales with social media is to reinforce advertising messages with a "zero moment of truth" (ZMOT)—a shared word-of-mouth experience.

14. **Flip the Funnel:** The secret to unlocking sales with social media is to harness your happy customers as a volunteer sales force, deploying them as your premier new customer acquisition team. Retention is the new acquisition.

15. **Interest Pays:** The secret to unlocking sales with social media is to sell to peoples' passions and interests—a key motivator for sharing.

16. **Sell Shovels:** The secret to unlocking sales with social media is marketplace thinking—create a social space for buyers and sellers to interact and transact with each other.

17. **Shopping First, Social Second:** The secret to unlocking sales with social media is to deploy social technology to help people solve shopping problems—finding, researching, deciding, buying, and enjoying.

18. **Sell to Niche Markets:** The secret to unlocking sales with social media is to sell to market niches—and build loyalty among people with a passion for what you sell.

19. **Get Rated. Get Reviewed:** The secret to unlocking sales with social media is to enable customers to share ratings and reviews about you and what you sell.

20. **Go Mobile:** The secret to unlocking sales with social media is to offer social utility with mobile technology—helping people shop smarter together.

P-SQUARED

As will be become apparent, the chapters of *The Social Commerce Handbook* have been written by two different authors with two very different styles. We're both called Paul, and we're both editors of *Social Commerce Today*, but we've each brought a different set of experience, insights, and styles to the social commerce table. One of us, Paul Chaney, is a seasoned social media consultant to business—from small local enterprises to major internationals, while the other, Paul Marsden is a consumer psychologist specializing in digital technology, brand communication, and shopper marketing. We've each selected our personal top 10 insights and examples from the world of social commerce.

What we both share is the belief that social commerce has the power to transform the world of commerce by humanizing it, democratizing it, and making it better. Commerce is essentially a social—human—activity involving interaction and transactions between a buyer and a seller. Social commerce humanizes commerce by putting people, not products, at the heart of commerce. Social commerce enables buyers and sellers to connect, collaborate, and work together toward their shared collective interests.

Social commerce also democratizes commerce, allowing more people than ever before to trade. And that is a good thing, because commerce connects people, bridges divides, breaks down barriers, and forges cooperative networks of interdependence. When commerce happens, it's not only money and goods that get exchanged but ideas too. And when ideas get exchanged, they get recombined and evolve, like cultural genes—driving technology, innovation, and even knowledge, forward. When you participate in social commerce, you are participating in the social evolution of humankind.

We think that's cool.

PLAY THE IMPULSE GAME

The only way to get rid of a temptation
is to yield to it.
—OSCAR WILDE

THE PERFUME RING

Sophie has just made an impulse purchase: a cocktail ring from fashion designer Oscar de la Renta. It was a Facebook exclusive, an offer made only to fans of the brand. And it cost just $65, a fabulous price considering that you won't get much change from $1,000 for the typical Oscar de la Renta creation.

The ring itself was special, containing a solid concentration of Esprit d'Oscar, the brand's recently launched signature fragrance, a delicate citrus-sandalwood perfume capturing "the essence of femininity—re-imagined." With runway credentials, the perfume ring had been featured on the fingers of fashion models showcasing de la Renta's latest collection.

So when Sophie, a dedicated follower of fashion, discovered in her Facebook news feed that Oscar de la Renta had opened a temporary pop-up shop on its Facebook Page to sell the perfume ring, she clicked through and bought on impulse.

COMMERCE MINDSET

In the world of commerce, the "impulse purchasing" is huge. Specifically, 40 percent huge. Around 40 percent of everything we buy is the result of an unpremeditated, spur-of-the-moment emotional impulse. An impulse purchase happens whenever we buy spontaneously and opportunistically based on emotional appeal. We may like to think of ourselves as level-headed, rational shoppers. But retailers know better. They know we are impulsive and emotional, and that as a result, our purchases are often unintended, unreflective, and unplanned.

Impulse purchasing is especially good news for buying through social media because, right now, very few people are actually using social media specifically *for* shopping. Like Sophie, most people use social media to connect and communicate with the people in their lives, not for shopping. So while shopping and connecting are not mutually exclusive—indeed, shopping can often be the excuse for socializing—social media has yet to be strongly associated with shopping. This means that in order to sell with social media, you have to face the prospect of selling to people not looking to buy. And the easiest way to do that is to sell a product or service that is typically bought on impulse.

So how do you go about selling on impulse with social media? To help, we can look at what's known about impulse buying. First, who buys on impulse? While we all buy on impulse from time to time, research shows that some people tend to be far more susceptible than others:

Women
Under 40 years old
Affluent
With disposable income
Enjoy shopping
Individualistic
Materialistic
Looking for self-betterment

If a number of these characteristics describe your customers, then social commerce may well work for you. These traits describe people who tend to buy on impulse, some of them compulsively. In extreme cases, they may even have a condition known as CBD (compulsive buying disorder) and may become "onomaniacs" (literally, insane shoppers). But to a greater or lesser degree, we're all susceptible to buying on impulse. There's even a simple and free test you can take to find out just how susceptible you are to impulse purchasing—it's called the "Impulse Buying Scale."[1]

Insights from commerce also tell us what kind of products tend to be bought on impulse, that is, the kind of products you should be selling through social media. Impulse purchases tend to be products with one or more of the following characteristics:

Products that make us feel good
Products that offer us good value
Products that make us look good

Products that make us feel good are known as *hedonic goods*: experiential purchases that offer fun, fantasy, pleasure, or excitement. From the impulse buy of a chocolate bar at the supermarket checkout to the purchase of a credit to play a Facebook game, hedonic purchases are usually unnecessary and discretionary from a purely functional perspective. But they tend to have emotional utility and offer sensorial rewards. In other words, they make us feel better. Think flowers, music, fragrances, feel-good movies, games, and comfort food. Or a perfume ring. Do you sell any such products? If so, selling with social media could work for you.

There's a second class of product that also tends to be purchased on impulse: goods presenting themselves as exceptionally good value. Even when people are not shopping, we are heavily influenced by a consumer culture that works on the principle of value maximization. This means that we are constantly trying to get more for less in pretty much everything we do: work, life, love, and, yes, shopping. When more is offered for less, even when we're not shopping, we buy on impulse. And that's why Sophie felt an irresistible urge to buy the $65 designer ring from a designer known for his $1,000+ price tags.

Generally speaking, what all this means is that selling with social media is most likely to work when you offer some kind of deal or promotion to trigger an impulse buy. But the smart trick is to think outside the price/volume box. It's not just about offering more product for less money, but about offering *more benefit for less cost*. And benefits and costs come in a number of distinct flavors:

economic, functional, psychological, and social. So think about how you could offer something extra that would be useful or helpful to your customers immediately, or would make them feel better about themselves or the people they care about.

SOCIAL MINDSET

In addition to products that make us feel good and that offer exceptional value, impulse buys include purchases that make us look good to others. A perfume ring from a fashion designer is worn not just for personal enjoyment; it is worn to make us look good. From a social mindset, this kind of impulse purchase has symbolic value and social utility insofar as it helps us communicate to others who we are and what we stand for. It helps us stand out from the crowd as individuals or fit in as members of groups with which we identify. If you wear Oscar de la Renta, that says something about you. It's a status symbol that has social utility in the form of badge value, signaling to others position, membership, and rank in a social hierarchy. Many fashion, luxury, sports, and music purchases are made as much for their social utility in managing a public image as they are for personal enjoyment. Do you, or could you, sell products that could be used for personal "image management"? Such products are particularly susceptible to being purchased on impulse and are, therefore, well suited to being sold though social media.

From a social mindset, there's one further impulse purchasing opportunity to consider. Often the social value of our purchases, the ability to make us look good to others, is not limited to what we buy, but *how* we buy. A product that has little intrinsic symbolic value, for example, diapers, can have real social currency when others don't have access. As we'll see in the chapter on Scarcity, when the diaper brand Pampers began selling from its Facebook page, it sold at impressive rate of over 1,000 packs an hour. The secret? The new line was not yet available elsewhere; Pampers was offering a Facebook exclusive.

In doing this, Pampers wasn't really selling diapers; rather, the brand was selling social utility in the form of get-it-first bragging rights. In other words, a social-first sales strategy can turn a commodity product into a prestige buy that triggers an impulse purchase. This can make the words "exclusive," "limited," and "special edition" strong impulse purchase triggers. The bottom line is that even if you're not in the business of helping people look good, you can stimulate impulse purchases with social media by offering social media exclusives.

UNLOCKING SOCIAL COMMERCE SALES

In summary, the first secret to unlocking the sales potential of social commerce is to focus on selling impulse purchases. These tend to be products that make people either feel good, look good, or get good value. They also tend to offer instant gratification at a relatively low price point.

While we're all susceptible to buying on impulse, some of us are more so than others. Younger women who love shopping and who have disposable income, who are ambitious, individualistic, and materialistic may be particularly prone to making impulse purchases.

Consider the following opportunities for unlocking sales with social media:

- People don't tend to use social media to shop (yet), so your social commerce success will largely be determined by your ability to sell unplanned and emotionally driven impulse purchases. What impulse purchases do you already sell? Consider these first as candidates for selling through social media.
- Specifically, consider how you could sell any products that *make people feel good* by offering fun, pleasure, fantasy, or excitement.
- And explore selling goods that *make your customers look good*, such as aspirational status symbols that have social currency.
- Products most likely to be purchased on impulse are also those that offer some kind of instant gratification. What digital products, digital bonuses, or digital discounts that offer immediate reward could you offer?
- Do you sell any products to younger women with disposable income who love shopping? This target group may be particularly susceptible to impulse purchasing.
- Impulse purchases also tend to be small-ticket items that don't require thought and evaluation in terms of long-term consequences. What low-cost products or services could you consider selling through social media?

INVOLVE THEM

We must become the change we want to see.

—Mahatma Gandhi

WHITE VINEGAR

Did you know that white vinegar is a miraculous cleaning product? You can use it to clean countertops, cooking appliances, grills, glass, sink fixtures, and more. It deodorizes trash cans, refrigerators, and bathrooms, and it removes stains from crockery, cutlery, plastic containers, and even carpets.

In fact, any major cleaning brand would be crazy not to have a white vinegar product. Or that's what Melanie thinks. It's also precisely what Melanie has told Unilever, the consumer goods giant with a range of big cleaning brands including Persil, Cif, and Domestos, via its Facebook page.

Melanie is a member of Unilever's online consumer advisory board that runs on Facebook. The advisory board is made up of consumer volunteers who regularly offer advice and ideas on Unilever innovation and marketing. In return, advisors get staff pricing on Unilever products from an online coupon store on Facebook, as well cash prize rewards for smart ideas. It works for Melanie *and* it works for Unilever. The company gets closer to its customers, and consumer advisors get products and promotions they want.

But there is something more than a quid pro quo transaction going on here. Melanie's involvement with Unilever means she feels like she's part of the company, which means she *cares* about it. And that psychological involvement means she buys Unilever brands when she can and she recommends them to her friends.

COMMERCE MINDSET

There is commercial value in involvement; emotional and mental investment makes things appear more personally important and relevant, and that drives affinity and loyalty. And when involvement also requires time and energy, we value it even more. It's what the *Harvard Business Review* calls "the IKEA Effect": the time and energy we invest in hex-keying together flat-packed pieces of semidisposable furniture results in us valuing the result more than we rationally should.[1] It's a spin on the classic "add an egg" insight that accelerated the sales of instant cake mixes back in the 1950s. By adding an (entirely unnecessary) egg to a cake mix, housewives became involved in the creation of the cake. It became *their* cake.

Creating a sense of ownership through involvement by getting customers to "add an egg" is a very powerful sales technique. Want to know the secret to the success of most successful TV franchise in the history of broadcasting, *American Idol*? One word: involvement. The people in the audience do much more than just watch; they are involved by "adding an egg" through weekly voting on who gets to stay and who gets to go. Want to know why the pharmaceutical industry works with armies of physicians to conduct late-stage clinical trials for new drugs? Same reason: involvement. Advisory involvement transforms sceptical physicians into enthusiastic and loyal promoters. For software companies running "beta" tests with lead customers, it's as much about involvement as it is about bugs; through preliminary testing, their software becomes *your* software.

But the solution to selling with involvement is perhaps best illustrated by a curious incident that happened nearly a century ago in a factory just outside Chicago. It involved selling ideas rather than products, but it demonstrates the "add an egg" power of involvement beautifully.

In 1924, researchers from MIT and Harvard University were called in to investigate how they could improve working conditions and productivity at a factory owned by Western Electric in Cicero, Illinois. The researchers arrived at the Hawthorne Works factory to find a huge complex of 45,000 workers assembling telephones and other consumer electronics. They decided to run a few experiments, inviting different workers to get involved in various tests of new working conditions. Would brighter lighting improve worker satisfaction and productivity, or would softer lighting be better? Would shorter working hours or longer hours with overtime be better?

What the researchers found completely confounded them.

Those workers who had been involved with testing brighter lighting preferred the new conditions, and their productivity went up. But those involved with testing softer lighting preferred those conditions, and their productivity went up! The researchers reran the tests, this time with even brighter and softer lighting. Same result. *Involvement in a test led to preference for whatever was tested.* This turned out to be the case for variations in working hours, as well. The lesson was this: involve workers in contrasting tests and both groups will prefer the test they've been involved with.

After much scratching of heads and reruns, the researchers finally realized that what was happening had nothing to do with changes in working conditions and everything to do with psychological involvement. By involving groups of workers in the test, they invested in an outcome and became psychologically involved with it. In other words, the researchers inadvertently but effectively "sold" workers on change in their workplace not by argument, but through involvement. The researchers dubbed this sales effect of involvement the "Hawthorne Effect" after the name of the factory, and this principle has since been demonstrated countless times over.

Whether you call it the Hawthorne effect, the power of involvement, the IKEA Effect, or the "add an egg" principle, the commercial implication is clear. Involve your customers as advisors or contributors and you will create loyal enthusiasts.

SOCIAL MINDSET

Creating ownership, affinity, and loyalty with involvement is commercially valuable, but from a social mindset you want more than this. You want active advocates who use their social influence and enthusiasm to bring in new customers. You want selling that is social, not personal. In other words, you aren't just selling to individuals, you're selling to individuals and their friends. Social selling is about making the sale in such a way that customers come back for more and bring their friends. The good news is that involvement works as a powerful social selling technique too. It not only creates loyal fans, it creates "super-fans" who enthusiastically promote you to their friends and work as unpaid but highly effective business ambassadors.

For example, take the curious history of 3M Post-it Notes. The little yellow stickies were initially a commercial flop. A 3M researcher had invented them for personal use, to create sticky bookmarks for his hymnal at choir practice, and he thought they were a great idea. Unfortunately, the world did not agree, and after a test launch, Post-it Notes were declared a failure.

Before pulling them from the market, however, 3M decided to send out boxes of unsold Post-it Notes to office workers all over America—not to sell them the product, but to ask for advice on how to market them. Treating consumers as advisors was unusual. But it worked. Not only did 3M receive useful feedback from its market outreach, but they also got sales—lots of them. Enamoured with a company that was actually listening to them and treating them as partners rather than targets, office workers started advocating Post-it Notes to their colleagues with a vengeance. Before long, Post-it Notes were spreading through the offices of corporate America like a virulent virus.

By involving customers as advisors, 3M had not only created an army of loyal fans but also a battalion of advocating super-fans. And these super-fans turned Post-it Notes from flop to sales phenomenon, and the little yellow stickies became the third biggest selling office supplies product in North America.

UNLOCKING SOCIAL COMMERCE SALES

Involvement is the secret to unlocking sales on social commerce. And this is precisely what Unilever has done by using Facebook to run an online consumer advisory board. Consumers get to vote, *American Idol*–style, and call the shots on Unilever's innovation and marketing. By involving their consumers in this way, the manufacturer creates super-fans for its brands who act as a volunteer sales force.

Unilever is not alone in harnessing the power of involvement in social media to unlock sales. For example, Modify Watches, a California start-up selling fun fashion watches, uses a free Facebook app to involve fans with prize brainstorming contests on product names, designs, colors, and packaging. The app, available from Boulder-based Napkin Labs is called, naturally enough, Brainstorm, and can be installed on any Facebook page with a single click. Modify Watches uses this app to harness the power of involvement and turn passive fans into super-fans who actively promote the brand.

Boston brewer Samuel Adams also uses involvement to sell with social media, running "crowdsourcing" events for its Facebook fans to vote on the characteristics—color, clarity, body, taste, and finish—of new beers. The custom app installed on the Sam Adams Facebook page is popular and has chalked up 142,000 "Likes" with events designed to create fans who are not only loyal adopters but super-fans who are enthusiastic advocates. Big brands are getting in on the act too. Harley Davidson, Intel, Pepsi, Coca-Cola, Home Depot, Nestlé, and Bobbi Brown Cosmetics are just some of the brands using involvement to sell with social media.

Of course, Facebook is not the only platform available for customer involvement. Proprietary-branded online communities can also be valuable real estate to foster customer involvement. For example, in 2011 Nestlé launched an innovative new social marketplace called Nestlé Marketplace, which allows consumers to discover, shop, and share 72 Nestlé brands. But that's not all Nestlé is up to with the site. The company also engages Marketplace customers as brand advisors, inviting them to share ideas and suggestions for new products, packaging, and usage occasions.

Computer manufacturer Dell has been doing something similar for some time with its IdeaStorm microsite. Through this site, Dell customers can suggest ideas for new features and products and, to date, nearly 500 of these suggestions have been implemented. Starbucks has followed Dell's lead and created My Starbucks Idea, a microsite where customers can share ideas on improving the Starbucks experience. Customers can also discuss ideas with each other and see how Starbucks is putting top ideas into action.

Another variation on the use-involvement-to-unlock sales solution comes from T-shirt design company Threadless. Threadless uses customer involvement in

Idol-style talent contests where T-shirt designers compete for customer "Likes." Only the most popular designs go into production and on sale—and when they do, they always sell out.

Similarly, Domino's Pizza Australia lets its half-million Facebook fans decide what its next pizza should be. On successive days fans vote for their favorite crust, sauce, and toppings, with the most popular selection from each day added to the pizza menu.

These are all examples of what we call "empowered involvement" to unlock sales with social media. How might you unlock the sales potential of social media with this kind of involvement? These starter ideas will get you on the right track:

- Are you innovating right now? Could you harness the power of quick and easy "add an egg" customer involvement with a poll to give customers a say in what you do? Finance and monetize this with a special thank-you offer in social media.
- Could you engage your customers in a beta-test of a new product before it comes out, perhaps getting their feedback on how best to market it? But rather than give the product away, finance the initiative by selling the innovation at a special price.
- How about advertising? Could your customers vote on new advertising artwork or copy options?
- Think about charity work, social responsibility, or good corporate citizenship. How could you involve your social media followers in what you do and how you do it and turn fans into super-fans?
- Consider using your social media presence to set up and run a customer advisory board with regular "add an egg" polls to involve customers in your business. Finance and monetize the involvement with a "staff shop" for your special advisors.

- Explore how you might develop a new range of products with customer input—and commercialize them in a special social media store.
- How about creating an online "social suggestion board" where customers submit and vote on each other's ideas?

THE EXPERIENTIAL IMPERATIVE

Nothing ever becomes real
till it is experienced.

—JOHN KEATS

WIDESPREAD PANIC

When Josh saw Widespread Panic at the 2011 Austin City Limits festival, the experience blew him away. The band rocked, grooved, and riffed their way through a 25th Anniversary tour date to a sold-out crowd at Austin's new Moody Theater. You just had to be there, Josh told his friends; being part of the live experience, sharing classic band moments in the making with other fans, was truly amazing. Except that Josh *wasn't* there. He was over

1,000 miles away in a South Beach condo, tuning into a pay-per-view experience on Widespread Panic's Facebook page.

For a $5 "entrance fee" (using Facebook's virtual "Credits" currency or PayPal), Josh and thousands of other fans from 19 different countries logged on to experience the live gig. Together they chatted, commented, and shared moments, and as the conversations echoed around Facebook, the virtual crowd doubled in size. It was a Facebook experience worth talking about, and so fans did—and their talk brought in up to 50 percent of digital revenue for the gig.

COMMERCE MINDSET

From a commercial perspective, selling an "experience" in social media was smart because people are increasingly looking to buy experiences rather than things. In a landmark report in the *Harvard Business Review* called "Welcome to the Experience Economy," researchers have shown that smart and profitable selling now involves staging experiences, rather than simply pushing goods and services. With the commoditization of "stuff," people—especially those with disposable income—increasingly shop for experiences, not things. The proof of the experiential pudding is, of course, Apple Retail, one of the most successful retail operations on the planet.

The commercial opportunity here is to use social media as an experience delivery mechanism and social commerce as a way to monetize the experience. From this perspective, your goal is to stage a sensational, personal, and memorable experience, because in today's "experience economy," that is what sells. Of course, this is all fine and good if you are in the event or entertainment business—sports, movies, music, TV and gaming—where experiences are what you sell. But what if you sell traditional goods and services?

The general opportunity is to use social media to run retail *events*. In the world of traditional retail, this is known as "pop-up retail," which involves setting up temporary stores to support new product launches. For example, lifestyle brands such as Adidas and H&M, as well as musicians like Jay-Z and Kanye West, run pop-up retail events that "pop up" unexpectedly and in unexpected locations to sell their new gear. The goal of pop-up retail is to drive buzz and accelerate product uptake by delivering experiential events around new product introductions, often piggybacking on bigger events such as a music festival, awards ceremony, or sporting event.

For example, Adidas, the current king of pop-up retail, launched its "Ransom" and "Blue" design collections with six temporary pop-up shops in secret locations across Germany, Austria, and Switzerland, only communicating their whereabouts to fans on Facebook. Each store was designed to "pop up" in an unexpected location or venue for a few days or weeks, sell only a limited range of the new gear, and then disappear. These experiential stores created self-funding buzz for Adidas designed to accelerate product adoption. Created by experts in experiential retail, D'Art Design Gruppe, the Adidas pop-up stores were also designed to be quick, easy, and inexpensive to install. It only required a few hours and a single hex key to set up the unique "pop-up" Adidas experience.

If pop-up experiential retail makes sense in the world of bricks and mortar, then it makes even more sense online. The social commerce opportunity is to set up online pop-up stores in social media to promote new product launches. This is precisely what an increasing number of brands—Burberry, Chanel, Heinz, Sony, Nine West, Rachel Roy, and others—are doing by setting up temporary pop-up stores on their Facebook page to drive buzz and accelerate new product uptake.

SOCIAL MINDSET

So, if the secret to unlocking sales with social media is to stage experiential retail events, what insight can a social mindset offer? From a social perspective, your customer is not merely a customer; they are also the primary means for you to acquire another, new customer. When you sell socially, you're selling not only in the hope that they'll come back for more, but that they'll come back for more *and* bring their friends. And to do that, you need to offer an experience worth talking about.

When customers talk, they tend to talk about their personal experiences. In particular, they talk about personal experiences that are surprising because they are at odds with their expectations. We can stay silent when a great experience meets high expectations, but we can't resist speaking out when an otherwise unremarkable experience beats low expectations. In fact, research we have conducted with the Interpublic Communications Group has found that over two-thirds of all word of mouth can be explained by differences between experiences and expectations. *Word of mouth* is the result of experiences that *beat or miss* expectations. If the value of social commerce lies in customers who come back for more *and* bring their friends, then a key secret to social commerce is to offer a customer experience that beats expectations.

Fortunately, we have a pretty good idea of where key customer expectations lie: with the familiar "Big Five"— price, quality, speed, service, and empowerment (control).[1] So your best bet for unlocking sales with social media is to focus on these five expectations and run experiential events designed to deliver expectation-beating experiences.

UNLOCKING SOCIAL COMMERCE SALES

Experience is the secret to unlocking sales with social media. So understand yourself not as a retailer but as a stage manager who stages remarkable retail events. Make your experiential retail events sensational, personal, and memorable and your customers will come back for more—and bring their friends with them.

This is exactly the kind of experience that is offered by event-based shopping clubs such as Gilt Groupe, Rue La La, Beyond The Rack, and Vente-Privée. These online retailers run regular time-limited "flash sale" events selling designer goods at knock-down prices.

Another experiential social commerce example is Sugar Inc., a content and commerce company, which holds live shopping events on its PopSugar online TV channel. Presented by PopSugar TV Host Allison McNamara, the events showcase 25 hand-selected gifts from the popular PopSugar 100 Gift Guide. Viewers also get the chance to win exclusive items throughout the broadcast. If it sounds like TV shopping, it is, but it's also interactive with a live chat feature allowing people to chat amongst themselves and with the presenters.

The bottom line is that if you are looking to unlock sales with social media, you'll need to deploy social media as event media and run shared and sharable experiential events. In other words, think of social commerce as e-commerce-enabled event marketing, not an e-commerce store in social media or an e-commerce store with social widgets. Your best bet is to take a leaf out of the pop-up retail book and use your social media pages to stage digital pop-up retail events that are simple, quick, and inexpensive to set up and run but deliver an experience that is worth talking about.

How can you unlock the sales potential of social media with remarkable retail events? Here are some ideas to get you thinking:

- Do you already run or sponsor events? Consider using social media to stream and share the experience and monetize it with an event store or virtual entrance fee.
- What new products or services are you going to be offering in the next 12 months? Could you stage a launch event in social media and allow guests to buy directly from where it is streamed?
- Compare yourself to the competition experientially: Bain reports that 80 percent of senior management believes their brands deliver a better experience. Only 8 percent of their customers agree.
- If you advertise, could you reveal your new campaign in social media first through an experiential online event monetized with a campaign store selling campaign merchandise?
- Search online for reports and case studies of successful pop-up retail ventures. How could you adapt these traditional pop-up retail events to the social media environment?
- Explore the possibility of creating an online experiential pop-up store in social media around a calendar event that's popular with your fans, such as a holiday or a sporting event.

- Consider how you might surprise and delight your fans with a special "fan event" in social media selling limited editions that are only available in social media.
- Do you have access to any experts, commentators, or celebrities? Consider showcasing them as hosts or performers during a live event streamed in social media.

INCENTIVIZE INTELLIGENTLY

Call it what you will, incentives are
what get people to work harder.

—NIKITA KHRUSHCHEV

THE ENCHANTED FOUNTAIN

Deborah wants an Enchanted Fountain. All her friends
have one. And she should be able to afford it: they only
cost $2.

Two dollars in YoCash, that is—virtual cash for the
Facebook-based game YoVille from social network game
developer Zynga. The Enchanted Fountain would make a
nice water feature for Deborah's virtual home in YoVille, a
personalized space in Facebook and a digitally simulated

environment in which she can entertain and interact with others.

The problem is that Deborah doesn't have any virtual cash left for her Enchanted Fountain. Of course, she could buy some more virtual case from Facebook in exchange for real cash. Zynga would like that, and so would Facebook, where most Zynga games are played. The two companies split the revenue 30/70 for such transactions: Facebook's 30 percent cut contributes about 10 percent to its entire revenue, which was nearly half a billion dollars in 2011.

Fortunately for Deborah, Zynga is running a half-price promotion on Enchanted Fountains and other virtual goods. But the sale is only running for 48 hours, and the deal is only applied if she and other players get together and buy in bulk. It's just the incentive Deborah needs, so she purchases virtual cash for real cash, prepurchases an Enchanted Fountain, and then contacts her friends and encourages them to do likewise. And it works. The minimum sales threshold for the deal is quickly reached and Deborah's Enchanted Fountain is delivered—along with 300,000 other virtual items sold in this 48-hour group-buy promotion that nets Zynga nearly a quarter of a million dollars in nonvirtual, real hard currency.

COMMERCE MINDSET

Unless you happen to be into gaming, the global $2.9 billion market for virtual goods—nonphysical objects purchased for use in online games—may be somewhat mystifying. But there's no mystery to Deborah's reaction to the group-buy incentive: it worked and she made a purchase. Incentives and "incentivization" are key to a commercial mindset; customers buy when they are incentivized to do so. The entire promotions business is built on this simple insight.

"Incentives are the cornerstone of modern life," writes Steven Levitt in the business bestseller *Freakonomics: A Rogue Economist Explores the Hidden Side of Everything.* The book recommends that we ditch Alexander Dumas's famous advice "cherchez la femme" (look for the woman) when trying to explain why people do things and, instead, look for the incentive behind the behavior. Somewhat irreverently, we like to call this "cherchez la carrotte" (look for the metaphorical carrot, which may or may not involve a woman).

While Levitt focuses mainly on how incentives (carrots) and disincentives (sticks) can lead to unintended consequences, his book makes the important point that incentives are not only economic in nature. Some are moral; norms we adhere to primarily because our conscience gives us grief if we don't. And others, as we'll see in a few paragraphs, are social incentives, in the form of group acceptance and inclusion.

As it happened, the particular incentive offered by Zynga was economic, but with a social twist: Deborah could get something for less if others bought too. It was a "social-buying" incentive, also known as "group-buy," "team buying," or "collective buying." While we tend to dismiss this kind of incentive as a marketing gimmick used by local deal sites such as Groupon, genuine group-buying is a powerful commercial force in China and is called *Tuángòu* (pronounced *twangoo*).

Typically, Tuángòu team-buys involve potential buyers seeking each other out on online bulletin boards and then nominating one person to negotiate a volume discount with a supplier. There are times, however, when participants will decide to "flash mob" a retailer, turning up in large numbers and demanding an on-the-spot group discount. More often than not, the retailer happily trades reduced margin for increased revenue; 50 televisions sold at a 5 percent margin is worth more than 5 sold at 15 percent.

In the West, the commercial potential of Tuángòu team-buying for businesses and their customers has yet to be fully realized. This is partly, we think, because the concept has been hijacked and rather lamely implemented in the daily deals sector. But if we were to pick one big business opportunity in social commerce, it would be rei-magining Tuángòu team-buying and using social media as a platform for demand-led group purchasing.

Of course, there's more to economic incentives with a social twist than Tuángòu group discounts. The most common solution is to simply run a referral rewards offer. For example, Dropbox, the popular "hard disk in the cloud" service for online document storage, uses referral rewards to win 35 percent of all new Dropbox custom-ers. The secret to success, as with all successful referral rewards, is what is known as "two-side incentives"; offer-ing rewards to both referring customers and those being referred. Two-side incentives work because it takes the curse off shilling to friends; both parties are rewarded.

More generally, getting customers to sell for you by incentivizing them to do so through referral rewards can be a very effective and efficient way to sell. To dem-onstrate the power of social referrals, writers for the *Harvard Business Review* implemented a simple customer-get-customer referral program for a telephone company. Spending only $4 per customer, the company increased profits by $486,090 with a total outlay of just $31,500.[1] What's more, new customers acquired through referral programs tend to be more valuable than those acquired by marketing. For example, one German bank looked at the quality of customers brought in by referral programs and found they were 16 percent more valuable than other customers.[2]

What should be clear by now from a commercial mindset is that if you're not already running a customer referral program using social media, you probably should.

SOCIAL MINDSET

Economic incentives can be powerful, but they are not the only incentive game in town. When social scientists talk about incentives, they're typically referring to social incentives, what we call "peer pressure"—our motivation to conform to shared norms and behavior, complying with the shared rules and expectations of the groups with which we identify. Social incentives here are all about the promise of acceptance, with a flipside social disincentive of being rejected or ostracized. Both are very powerful motivators. The implication, from a social mindset, is that a powerful way of selling with social incentives in social media would be to sell products that have social incentives built-in because they help people fit in. In other words, products that have social utility. Must-have fashion accessories and team sports merchandise stand out as prime candidates.

But not all social incentives are about fitting in. Some are about precisely the opposite: they are about standing out. For example, there may be a social incentive to own an Enchanted Fountain precisely because others *don't* have one; the Enchanted Fountain becomes as status symbol signaling privilege and position in a social hierarchy. In other words, an Enchanted Fountain has social utility because it helps us stand out, and that's precisely why we want one. So another social commerce opportunity is to sell products with social media that have social utility because they are status symbols that help us stand out.

Finally, there's one other form of social incentive that you might use when selling in social media: helping people use their social intelligence—their ability to learn from each other and profit from social situations—when they are buying from you. Amazon is the king of this kind of social utility. It offers a suite of social shopping features to help people shop with their social intelligence: shared customer reviews, ratings, bestseller and recommendation lists, as well as a powerful "social recommender system" that makes personalized suggestions based on similarities between customer browsing, rating, and buying patterns. The opportunity for social commerce here lies in socially incentivizing sales with shopping features that help people shop smarter using their social intelligence.

UNLOCKING SOCIAL COMMERCE SALES

A powerful secret for unlocking sales via social commerce is to offer social incentives that either provide economic benefits socially, through group-buy or referral rewards, or offer purely social incentives in the form of helping customers fit in, stand out, or shop smarter with their social intelligence.

One interesting idea explored by Starbucks is to offer social incentives through its Facebook-fronted loyalty rewards program, in which members can pay on Facebook and gift coffee to a Facebook friend. The gift appears as a coupon code in a Facebook message that can be redeemed in-store. It's an interesting evolution of the customer-get-customer referral program. (What Starbucks is not doing yet, but probably should, is offer two-side incentives for this gifting via social media, for example, offering a bonus or saving to both parties.)

Another smart use of incentives in social commerce comes from American Express, which "sells" loyalty rewards by personalizing offers based on Facebook "Likes." You've clicked a Facebook "Like" button for wine, then your loyalty rewards will include wine. In an innovative twist, Amex supercharges this personalized incentive program by inviting its business customers (retailers) to offer Amex cardholders incentives for shopping with them. Amex aggregates, curates, and wraps these offers up as personalized rewards. Citibank, too, is experimenting with a similar incentive program on Facebook, allowing customers to give, share, and pool reward points from its "Thank You" rewards program.

These are all imaginative approaches to selling with incentives, but you don't need complex apps to profit from the power of incentives and unlock the sales potential of social media. For example, you could simply take a leaf from the book of Domino's Pizza, which uses the check-in app foursquare to reward customers with tasty deals when they check in to its locations. To get started consider, the following:

- How could you use group-buy deals in social media to incentivize purchase with discounts or, better yet, bonuses for customers who club together and buy in bulk?
- Explore how you could unlock sales with a social media referral program, rewarding two or more linked sales between friends. Remember that the secret to referral success is to offer two-sided incentives that reward all parties making the purchase.

- Investigate the possibility of offering social incentives in the form of access to new products in social media before you sell them elsewhere. By doing this you'll be offering your fans and followers bragging rights and activating their advocacy.
- Keep it simple. How could you attract new social media followers using incentives such as one-time promotion codes, coupons, or discounted shipping for those who follow you?
- Consider options for what to sell for incentivized social commerce. Successful selling may work best when social incentives are built into what you sell by helping your customers stand out or fit in. Think in terms of status symbols or items that signal group allegiance.
- How about creating a special club for your most valuable customers, those who buy more and recommend more, that offers extra benefits and incentives for loyalty and advocacy?
- Explore how you could sell with social incentives using social, mobile, and web apps that help your customers shop smarter with their social intelligence by learning from the tastes and experience of others.

SELL WITH SCARCITY

To my mind the old masters are not art;
their value is in their scarcity.

—THOMAS EDISON

DESPERATE FOR DIAPERS

Picture this: A young mom is chatting with a friend on Facebook and shopping is the furthest thing from her mind. But then she catches a status update from one of the brands she follows on Facebook. Pampers has just started a "flash sale" on its Facebook page, selling a limited quantity of its new "Cruisers" line of diapers before they hit the stores.

Her interest is piqued, and she shares the news with her friend, and they both click through to the Pampers pop-up store on Facebook. But there they find that the 1,000 packs of Cruisers on offer have already sold out. What is going on? They're just diapers!

Well, what was going on was that Procter & Gamble, the consumer goods giant behind Pampers, harnessed the power of *scarcity* to sell in social media. Scarcity sells because we want more of what others have less of.

COMMERCE MINDSET

In the world of commerce, one of the most sure-fire ways to shift stock is to tell customers that there is only a limited quantity available. To customers, the basic rule of supply and demand applies to "perceived value." When supply is short, value, as perceived by customers, is high. By making a limited quantity of a new range of diapers available, P&G increased the perceived value of what they were selling. And their result was an impressive rate of sales.

This commercial value of scarcity extends beyond consumer sales to business sales as well. For example, one case study reported in the *Harvard Business Review* recounts how a telephone sales team doubled wholesale orders for beef simply by announcing that beef was in short supply.[1] But what's particularly interesting about this case study was that it illustrated that we value scarce information as well as scarce resources. When the same wholesale beef sales team added that information about a beef shortage came from exclusive "insider" source, sales jumped by an astounding 600 percent. The commercial implications are clear: drive sales by telling customers it's an offer that others don't know about, *and* that there's a limited supply.

The commercial logic of selling with scarcity is baked into human psychology, and based on what's known as "FOMO:" Fear of Missing Out. FOMO is so powerful that it influences our own perceptions. FOMO means that, as toddlers, we prefer toys we can't have or that are taken away from us. As teens, FOMO means our love for a crush is strongest when our parents restrict or forbid access to our paramour (something that psychologists poetically call "The Romeo and Juliet Effect"). And, as adult consumers, FOMO means we prefer products and services when they are in scarce supply; even food will taste better when there is less of it available.[2]

P&G harnessed the power of FOMO and the commercial wisdom of scarcity not only through a limited flash sale, but also by selling through a "here today, gone tomorrow" temporary pop-up store on their Facebook page. Because pop-up stores are fleeting and ephemeral, their scarcity means they have enhanced perceived value with customers. Procter & Gamble brought pop-up retail to Facebook.

SOCIAL MINDSET

Scarcity makes sense not only from a commercial mindset, but also from a social mindset. People talk about scarce stuff. There is nothing so tempting as to spread a secret precisely because it's a secret. From a social mindset, the rationale for P&G's pop-up flash sale on their Facebook page was to get a new product into the hands of their fans *and* give them something to talk about. Why? Because word of mouth is particularly valuable during the launch phase of new product, primarily because word of mouth makes advertising more effective by adding a credible consumer voice into the communication mix.

Buying diapers online is not newsworthy in itself. But getting your hands on a new line of diapers before anyone else has conversational currency. By using scarcity to sell, P&G made the unremarkable remarkable. And in doing so, they turned the brand's Facebook fans into super-fans; fans who are not only loyal enthusiasts but also active advocates.

There's another advantage to selling in social media with scarcity: *social utility*. Much of what we buy is purchased because it has functional utility, that is, it solves a practical problem we're facing. However, many problems are not functional in nature but social. Basic social psychology reveals that people are preoccupied by two social problems: "How can I fit in and be loved, and how can I stand out and be respected?" In other words, problems of "social bonding" and "social status." These are the ultimate social questions we face. By selling with scarcity, P&G offered the ultimate social answer: enhanced social status along with bragging rights that come with getting something exclusive, early, and that's not available to others.

UNLOCKING SOCIAL COMMERCE SALES

P&G combined a commercial mindset with a social mindset to sell smart to fans in social media using the power of scarcity. The commercial power of scarcity helped shift stock, while the social power of scarcity as status-enhancing conversational currency turned brand fans into super-fans by activating their advocacy. It's the kind of smart selling you'd expect from P&G.

But the consumer goods giant has not been alone in selling with scarcity in social media. Burberry, Gilt, Heinz, Nine West, Oscar de la Renta, Rachel Roy, and Unilever are just some of the other big brands selling with social media by offering their fans and followers exclusive VIP access to new, yet-to-be launched products through limited flash sales in social media.

The social commerce opportunity for your business is clear: use social commerce to offer social utility in the form of enhanced social status with limited editions and early access to new products. To help get you started, consider the following:

- Are you launching any new products in the coming months? If so, explore how you could offer your social media followers early access, even if it's just a week or so, via a pop-up store in social media.
- Explore the possibility of offering sharable coupons with social sales to help your customers share the word and bring in new customers.
- Remember, selling with scarcity is about FOMO (Fear of Missing Out); what could you do to heighten that fear of missing out on limited-volume or limited-time offers?
- From a social mindset, selling with scarcity is all about selling social utility in the form of social status (bragging rights through privileged access), so consider offering exclusive "insider" information along with what you sell (interesting facts, stories, or people behind the product) to reinforce the enhanced social status.
- Discuss the possibilities of offering daily, weekly, and monthly exclusives or limited editions that are only available via social media channels.

- When you sell through social channels, create a sense of urgency with limited quantity and limited time offers, and heighten the fear of missing out with special offer pricing.
- Are you running a marketing or advertising campaign? Consider selling exclusive campaign artwork and campaign merchandise through social media.

BUILD CONSISTENCY

A leader has to "appear" consistent.
That doesn't mean he has to be consistent.

—JAMES CALLAGHAN, FORMER BRITISH PRIME MINISTER

SMELLS LIKE FACEBOOK SPIRIT

"FITD" or "foot in the door": it's a classic sales technique. This approach helps a business get its metaphorical foot-in-the-door with a potential customer by first getting them to agree to a small request, like ordering a free sample, and then making a second bigger request, like buying a full-size version. Here's how this technique works on Facebook.

Alexis loves Burberry and is a huge fan of their products. But she's also a student, which unfortunately means she can rarely afford the latest designs from the British luxury fashion house. But Alexis does everything you'd expect from a true Burberry fan: she rents Burberry creations from online rental agencies such as Bag, Borrow, or Steal and Rent the Runway; follows Burberry on Facebook; and she pins her Burberry favorites for all to see on the social scrapbooking site, Pinterest.

Fortunately for Alexis, Burberry understands the value of fans, even temporarily impoverished fans, such as Alexis. So, in August 2011 the fashion house showed Alexis some fan-love in social media by offering fans a free sample of its yet-to-be-launched new fragrance, Burberry Body. Alexis, of course, ordered the fan-first exclusive.

Then, a few weeks later, after the public launch of Burberry Body, a pop-up fan store appeared on Burberry's Facebook page selling the fragrance itself. Alexis went right ahead and purchased the fragrance.

COMMERCE MINDSET

From a commercial perspective, what Burberry was doing was using the powerful principle of consistency to introduce the new fragrance to the brand's fans. By inviting fans to first order a free sample, and do so publicly on Facebook, Burberry increased the likelihood that fans would later buy the fragrance. The consistency principle works as a sales technique because we like to feel and be seen as consistent in what we say and do. Using the principle of consistency to sell can be remarkably effective, as has been illustrated by a famous field experiment conducted by psychologists back in 1966 in Palo Alto. Recounted by psychologist Robert Cialdini in *Influence: Science and Practice* (in our opinion, one of the best books available on social sales techniques), the experiment ended with an entire neighborhood agreeing to wreck their gardens and ruin their views with huge billboards.[1]

In this experiment, psychologists went undercover, posing as members of the "Community Committee for Traffic Safety." They knocked on the doors of residents in an affluent residential area in Palo Alto, California, and asked if they'd mind erecting huge "Drive Carefully" billboards on their front lawns. Not surprisingly, the vast majority of residents (83 percent) refused outright—except for those in one particular group.

In this group, 76 percent agreed to sacrifice their view to a billboard! The group wasn't made up of older or younger, more or less affluent, or even more or less civic-minded residents. In fact, all this group had in common was that two weeks prior, they had been selected at random, contacted, and asked if they'd put a small "Be a Safe Driver" car sticker on their cars—virtually all had agreed. Once the residents had made a public commitment to a small request, they felt a self-imposed pressure to conform to the large request based on expectations of consistency.

In the commercial world of sales, the pressure to appear to be consistent is used to upsell and cross-sell all the time. A smart sales associate will usually "presell" you a couple of different low-cost items first, but in doing so, get you to agree that each has a certain must-have feature. Then they'll upsell you to a much more expensive item that has both must-have features, and you'll buy it because you've already publicly agreed that the features are important. Simple but smart.

SOCIAL MINDSET

But what does this hard-nosed sales technique that plays on our desire to be consistent in what we say and do have to do with social selling? The answer is that the psychological motivation to be consistent is far higher in a social, shared environment; the pressure to be *seen to be consistent* can be more powerful than actually being consistent. So when Burberry runs a sampling campaign in Facebook, with orders being shared across newsfeeds, the brand increases the likelihood that each sample turns into a future purchase. Make commitment public, and consistency will follow, even if it costs. And by making the fragrance exclusively available to fans first, Burberry gave its fans an additional reason to talk and enthuse, making the initiative even more public.

It's smart social selling. And it fits well into an overall customer journey built on a series of small, consistent but cumulative steps, beginning with a seemingly trivial "Like" on a Facebook page. This small public demonstration of commitment to the brand seemingly costs nothing to fans, but it increases the probability that they'll order a free sample, which increases the likelihood they'll buy the perfume, which increases the likelihood they'll one day by a Burberry accessory, then a trench coat, and one day perhaps even something from the runway. In summary, the secret to unlocking sales with Facebook is a consistency-powered shared customer journey from a "Like" to "loyalty."

UNLOCKING SOCIAL COMMERCE SALES

Unlocking sales on social commerce means using the power of consistency to take social media followers on a journey involving steps of increasing commitment. From small acorn sales grow mighty oak sales.

One interesting illustration of the possibilities for using consistency to drive social commerce sales was a 2011 campaign by German car manufacturer BMW in the UK. BMW owners were invited to buy an exclusive, limited-edition car key cover for their BMW on Facebook. The price-point was low ($42), and the revenues insignificant for BMW. But the commerce campaign was smart social selling because it involved BMW owners making a public commitment to the brand, thereby increasing the chances that when the time came, that they'd purchase another BMW. The general implication for sales is evident: if you have the opportunity to sell low-cost branded merchandise through social media, do it, and incentivize customers to share news of their purchase. These small public purchases will pay back handsomely in terms of increased customer loyalty.

Blendtec, a company that makes very high-powered and equally high-priced commercial-grade blenders, used the power of consistency in another way. The company deployed the foot-in-the-door technique using entertainment to get people to do something that would be consistent with them later buying the brand; Liking or voting for their kooky YouTube video ads. The "Will it blend?" homemade ads, produced on a shoestring budget, featured CEO Tom Dickson grinding up any manner of things in a Blendtec blender—iPhone, garden rake, marbles, glow sticks, etc. The videos were viewed, Liked, and shared over 130 million times, and the company's sales jumped by over 700 percent. Just as a journey of a thousand miles begins with a single step, a sales jump of 700 percent begins with a single, consistent step—viewing, liking, or sharing an ad.

Another example of how consistency can be used to sell in social media is MyStarbucksIdea, a crowdsourcing site from Starbucks that collects customer ideas for product and service improvement. By asking customers for their ideas, Starbucks is inviting customers to act in a way that is consistent with caring about the brand, and thus buying from it. In addition, people submitting ideas to the site feel a sense of ownership in the brand and pride that they are helping to shape product development. Dell does something similar on its crowdsourcing site Ideastorm. Such feedback is consistent with caring, and caring is consistent with customer loyalty. It doesn't hurt that both companies have implemented and profited from many of the ideas that have been submitted.

Given the power of consistency, it might seem like a good idea to hide online deals and offers behind a "Like-gate" or "share-gate" and only allow access if a customer "Likes" you first. But there is a wrinkle. Psychologists have shown that when people feel forced or coerced into doing something, any subsequent pressure to be consistent evaporates. The power of the "Like" button as a sales-inducing tool relies on it being *voluntarily clicked*.

But overall, the message should be clear: a powerful secret to unlocking sales in social media is to sell using consistency through progressive and public upselling that takes a fan from "Like" to "Loyalty."

- Once you've collected Facebook "Likes" on your site or Facebook page, explore what could be the next small, easy step to move fans up the loyalty ladder. Possibilities include ordering a sample, downloading content or signing up for a newsletter.
- Consider what other bite-size experiences you could offer from your social media store or e-commerce site. Remember to make purchases or orders shareable.

- Think about how you might get fans to recommend you to their friends, even those fans who are not currently customers. The simple act of recommendation will make fans more likely to buy: their behavior will line up to be consistent with their words.
- Are there any opportunities to sell low-cost, branded merchandise or accessories from your social media pages? These purchases are consistent with, and, therefore, will increase the likelihood of future purchases.
- Once a customer makes an initial purchase, find ways to upsell add-on products; use incentives such as coupons or discounts.
- Think of ways to run an updated social commerce version of the classic loyalty-building contests found on the back of breakfast cereal boxes. For example, invite customers to submit (and share) an entry into a free prize drawing that involves offering a reason they most like your company or product.
- Consider the use of crowdsourcing for product development, naming new products or ways to improve customer experience; this could be facilitated either on a social media page, your own website, or standalone microsite.

RECIPROCITY RULES

I like to believe that love
is a reciprocal thing, that it can't
really be felt, truly, by one.

—SEAN PENN

CHICKEN SOUP FOR THE SOUL

You're home from work and your head hurts. You're tired, feverish, and it feels as if your eyes and throat are coated with sandpaper. No question about it: you've got a bout of seasonal flu, and you're miserable.

The doorbell rings and you're delivered a small package. It's from Heinz—a can of "Get Well" Chicken Soup with a personalized Get Well message from a friend on the can label! You feel a bit better already. You heat the soup, enjoy it, and then feel well enough to venture out to do some grocery shopping. And guess what? While roaming the supermarket aisles you pick up another can of Heinz soup.

When Heinz opened up a pop-up shop on its Facebook page during the flu season of 2011, the brand harnessed the powerful principle of reciprocity to sell its "get-well" soup.

COMMERCE MINDSET

Reciprocity has long been used as an effective sales technique: before asking a customer to buy, you offer them something free first. It might be some information, a free gift, or even a welcoming smile. Regardless of the fact that they never asked for anything upfront, they feel indebted to you and, therefore, will be more likely to buy from you. Charities use reciprocity all the time for fundraising, sending out unsolicited small gifts along with a donation request. This strategy is remarkably effective at turning would-be donors into actual donors, often doubling donation rates. And if you've ever bought a car, the salesman you dealt with probably used reciprocity to sell to you. Remember that time when you asked for a deal and the salesman said he didn't have the authority to offer you a discount, but that he'd ask his manager? He was doing you a favor, so when he came back with a slightly better price (probably not having talked to the manager at all) you felt obligated to buy. He'd done you a favor, so you felt the need to return the favor.

One famous example of how reciprocity can drive sales is recounted in the book *Influence: The Psychology of Persuasion,*[1] which describes how psychologists used reciprocity to sell raffle tickets. The psychologists went undercover on museum art tours posing as tour participants, and they began randomly offering to buy drinks for other tour participants. Only at the end of the tour did they try to sell their raffle tickets. They found that people were far more likely to buy if they had been offered a drink first. As the saying goes, there's no such thing as a free lunch or a free drink.

So how did Heinz use reciprocity to sell its soup on Facebook? The soup was sold for $3, meaning that nothing was offered up front for free as per the standard reciprocity sales trick. What Heinz was doing was far smarter. By making the Facebook store a *gift* store, Heinz ensured that someone was going to receive its soup for free—it was the flu-stricken friend receiving the surprise free gift. And what better time to receive a gift than when you're feeling unwell, especially if the gift makes you feel better.

So it was the gift recipients of the soup who felt the force of reciprocity and the desire to reciprocate. Of course, much of the urge to reciprocate would be directed toward the friend gifting the soup, but Heinz benefited, too, both by association and by the feel better effect of the warm soup. It was a smart social twist on the reciprocity sales technique, and one that is well worth emulating. So if you're looking to sell with social media, consider the inherently social gift store. It's an ideal fit with the social context of social media.

SOCIAL MINDSET

Through its pop-up social media gift store, Heinz found a smart way to sell itself into the homes and hearts of its fans' friends by using reciprocity. But the value of the social media sales campaign didn't stop there. When looked at from a social mindset, we see that the reciprocity included a dose of social utility. By gifting a can of get-well soup, customers strengthened their social bond with a friend. So Heinz was helping in a ritual of social bonding, one of the ultimate motivations behind much of our social behavior.

We don't want to overstate the case—it was only soup after all—but through the pop-up gift store on Facebook, Heinz was only superficially selling soup. What Heinz was really selling was social utility, helping people bond socially. Just as social bonding manifests itself in other primates by their peculiar habit of picking fleas from each other's fur coats, humans bond by gifting and gossiping. By participating in the enlightened self-interest of reciprocal altruism, a mere can of soup was playing a role in our social lives at a very profound level. Smart and very social.

UNLOCKING SOCIAL COMMERCE SALES

The Heinz case is delightful, smart, and possibly even visionary insofar as it gives a tantalizing partial glimpse of what one day might be possible through the creative use of digital gifting in social commerce. But how well did the soup sell?

Heinz sold one can of get-well soup to one in every eight of its Facebook fans. On the face of it, this 12.5 percent fan-to-customer conversion rate is not bad. But in reality, this only translated into rate-of-sale of about 500 cans per week, something a small supermarket would hope to achieve. To state the obvious, it obviously wasn't a big revenue generator for Heinz.

Of course, Heinz was hampered by the logistics and costs of sending out a heavy can of soup by post and personalizing the can label. A lighter, higher-margin product may have faired better—digital products, perfume, and cosmetics would have been ideal.

The sales from the Heinz campaign may seem disappointing, but they do in fact set a realistic expectation level for social media sales. What the Heinz campaign tells us is that a well-designed and executed pop-up sales campaign in social media might make a volume of sales equivalent to about 10 percent of your initial fan or "Like" count, and do so over four weeks. But by doubling the fan base from 16,000 to 32,810, the campaign itself helped ensure that any subsequent campaigns with similar effectiveness would deliver double the sales. If subsequent campaigns had a similar effect on fan growth, and the same proportion purchased, by the time Heinz was on its fifth campaign, it would be shipping 32,000 cans of soup.

When it comes to harnessing reciprocity to sell socially in social media, the Heinz pop-up gift store is not the only show in town. A smart alternative is employed by online shopping clubs such as Gilt and LivingSocial. These sites use simple social sharing buttons on product pages to encourage members to "gift" friends with news of exclusive offers. These informational gifts from friends trigger a desire to reciprocate, and the result is sign-ups and sales. The general opportunity for social commerce is to explore how you could use your social media channels as platforms for running a "social" referral program where your fans reward their friends.

One great example of social referrals is from the extended warranty provider Squaretrade, which offers the friends of existing customers $5 discount on their

purchases if they are referred in. In effect, existing customers get to gift $5 to their friends courtesy of Squaretrade.
The uninvited gift triggers a desire to reciprocate by signing up for a new warranty. Smart.

Similarly, men's clothier J. Hilburn has launched a
social referral program where it offers a $50 store credit
for the referrer and $50 off the first order for the person
who is referred. Customers can refer their friends through
Facebook, Twitter, and e-mail.

Another social commerce opportunity based on reciprocity that we're very bullish about, but that we've yet
to see realized, is "social sampling." When a customer
makes a purchase, they get to send a free sample to one
or two friends. The uninvited gift from a friend would be
a strong psychological incentive to purchase.

There are any number of opportunities for unlocking the sales potential of social media by harnessing the
power of reciprocity. Consider the following:

- Review the Heinz pop-up gift store campaign; are there any
  products that you sell that are particularly suited to gifting,
  especially seasonal or calendar event products? If so, consider
  selling a social media exclusive for gifting such as a limited
  edition or personalized edition.
- More generally, consider how you might sell more socially by
  helping people use gifting to reinforce social bonds.
- Empower your existing customers to become an effective
  volunteer sales force by allowing them to offer discounts to their
  friends and family through a social referral program.
- From the commerce mindset, reciprocity is all about giving first,
  taking later. Explore what you could give to your fans up front, or
  how you could help them solve a problem. They'll pay you back
  with loyalty.

- Think, from a social mindset, how else you might allow your fans to help their friends in a way that leads to a sign-up or purchase. For example, consider "social sampling" that would enable fans to send free samples to their friends. Or explore the possibility of a social referral program, where fans can personally reward friends with offers for signing up or buying.

SOCIAL VALIDATION

*A wise man learns from the experience
of others, a fool by his own.*

—LATIN PROVERB

THE GOOD GIG

Have you checked your "event feed" lately? You'll find
your own personal event feed via a Facebook app from
online ticketing service Ticketmaster. The app lists
upcoming events you might like to attend based on the
events and music that you and your friends like and listen to on Facebook. And, of course, the app lets you buy
tickets for those events. The app filters by location and

popularity, and, of course, supports in-app purchasing of e-tickets. The Ticketmaster app is social, personal, and a glimpse into the future potential of social e-commerce. And it's built around the powerful concept of "social validation."

COMMERCE MINDSET

It's one of the oldest sales techniques in the book: if you want to sell, show people that others are buying. When people are unsure of what to do or buy, they'll assume that others around them know what they're doing or buying, so they do likewise. Seeing someone else buy something you are considering "socially validates" that option as a good choice. So the sales trick is to create the illusion that your product is popular and in-demand. Do that and you'll sell more. Of course, the simplest way of social validating what you sell is to tell people that it's the "industry standard," "market leader," or "most recommended" product. If they believe you, you'll shift stock. By offering social validation for what you are selling, you are giving people social proof that the product that you are promoting is the smart choice.

Social validation, a term that was popularized by Dr. Robert Cialdini,[1] is what psychologists call "informational social influence." People copy from and conform with one another, both deliberately and automatically, based on an implicit assumption that others have the accurate information needed to act correctly. (The other type of social influence is "normative social influence," which happens when we are influenced by a desire to be *liked*, rather than to be *right*).

The Ticketmaster app uses social validation to sell by creating a personal feed of curated events that have been validated by friends and other users of the app. This social information provides "social proof" that certain events on offer are worth attending.

Amazon has been using social validation to sell since it first opened. User ratings and reviews, popularity lists, and a "social recommender" system (people who viewed that, viewed this) all work to together to socially validate what's on sale. This kind of social validation can boost sales by about 10 percent, according to software companies selling Amazon-style social validation features for e-commerce sites.[2]

But what's particularly smart about the Ticketmaster app is that it makes social validation personal; it validates options based on personal tastes and the tastes of friends on Facebook.

SOCIAL MINDSET

The Ticketmaster event feed app is social by design. Not only does it have standard Facebook sharing features built in, but it also offers users "social utility" in the form of enhanced social intelligence, helping them shop smarter by learning from the actions and experiences of others. This kind of social learning is the smartest kind of intelligence.

It so happens that we humans are almost entirely unique in our ability to learn socially. Most other animals must learn via trial and error, whereas humans can learn from the mistakes and successes of other people.

Social is smart. As the saying goes, "a wise man learns from the experience of others, a fool by his own." The business opportunity here is to use social validation to help shoppers shop smarter. By helping shoppers shop smart through social learning, you are giving them an extra reason to shop with you.

Using social validation to sell also helps drive new business: one customer's purchase can be used to validate another customer's decision. The trick is to use social media to make your customers' purchases visible to one another. By making a sale public, you socially validate what you're selling and therefore are half way to making another sale.

Social validation works in a similar way to word of mouth, but it uses behavior rather than words to add credibility and legitimacy for what you are selling. Seeing someone else purchase something can be far more powerful than having them explain why you should purchase it. Actions speak louder than words.

UNLOCKING SOCIAL COMMERCE SALES

The secret to unlocking sales with social media is to get the products that you sell validated socially by the purchases, endorsements, and behavior of others. Social validation delivers social utility; it allows consumers to shop smarter using their social intelligence and to learn from the actions of others. The general social commerce opportunity is to turn your social media channels into platforms that can help one another shop smart by learning from each other.

For example, social commerce website ShopSocially provides a pristine example of how retailers can take advantage of social validation for building branding and increasing sales. The site promises to "turn 10–40 percent of your shoppers into brand ambassadors, increase engagement on Facebook and website by up to 30 percent to drive brand impressions and incremental clicks to [the retailer's] online store." The mechanism used by the site is to incentivize customers to share their purchases with friends on Facebook and Twitter, as well as through e-mail.

Wireless Emporium, an online retailer of cell phone accessories, shows shoppers names, faces, and commentary from satisfied customers. When the site finds that friends of a shopper have made purchases from the store in the past, it highlights that activity, making it more conspicuous.

Back in 2010, Levi's launched a "Friends Store" on its e-commerce site. The Friends Store allowed visitors to log in using their Facebook credentials and see what their friends had "Liked." Following Levi's lead, Estée Lauder integrated its Smashbox e-commerce site with Facebook in order to provide visitors with instant personalization and socialization options. On Smashbook, potential customers can see the overall most "Liked" (socially validated) products as well as those products that their friends have liked.

Another example of how to sell with social validation is through the use of online communities. Procter & Gamble has done this numerous times with sites like Super Savvy Me and Pampers Village. These proprietary communities allow members to learn from each other in order to make smarter shopping decisions. What these brands are doing successfully is asking the right question. It is not, "How can I sell smarter with social media?" It is "How can I help my customers shop smarter with social media?"

Helping people shop smart with their social intelligence by socially validating options on offer doesn't mean you have to emulate Ticketmaster and develop sophisticated e-commerce apps. Basic social media functionality can suffice. For example, Facebook offers a range of free and easy-to-use social plug-ins for e-commerce sites that add social validation in the form of Likes, comments, and recommendations on product pages. Likewise, a range of social plug-ins are available from other software companies such as Bazaarvoice, 8thBridge, and Reevoo that add additional social validation into your e-commerce mix in the form of share buttons, ratings, reviews, and comments.

Consider the following to make a start in selling socially with social validation:

- Review your sales copy; do you use the social validation that is implicit in the terms "industry standard," "market leader," "bestseller," "fastest growing," "most recommended," or "most popular," etc.? If not, update your copy with this simple kind of social validation.
- Focus social selling efforts on those products that are already most "socially validated" because they are the "industry standard," "market leader," "fastest selling" etc.
- Systematically invite your customers to share the products they like, want, and have purchased.
- Consider deploying Facebook's free social plug-ins on the product pages of your e-commerce site, or use a third-party solution such as 8thBridge or Bazaarvoice.
- Most important, put yourself in the shoes of your customers. What is the reason to buy from your Facebook store or

e-commerce website? How could you help them shop with their social intelligence by helping them learn from each other's actions and experiences?

ARM YOURSELF WITH AUTHORITY

Believe one who has proved it.
Believe an expert.

—Virgil, Roman Poet

WWSJD?

"What Would Steve Jobs Do?" That's the mantra of Dan, a web designer from South Beach. And it's the first thing Dan asks himself when taking on a new design project. Asking himself what the late design-obsessed CEO of Apple would have done is a little mental trick that gets Dan into his design groove.

Dan may be good with pixels, but he's certainly no authority on how real-world molecules stack up to make good design. Yet his friends expect him to be design savvy in *everything*. So Dan has a secret. It's called Fab, a hip, private, and members-only shopping club that offers design inspiration from experts with daily design deals at up to 70 percent off. With Fab, Dan not only gets to discover great products with great design, but by sharing what he discovers, he gets to be known as someone who knows about good design. Fab is his secret source of design cred.

COMMERCE MINDSET

Selling with authority is one of the most powerful techniques in commerce. Don't sell it yourself; let experts do the work for you. Software company SAP sells its software using the borrowed authority of industry leaders with its campaign "the best run companies run on SAP" sales message. The Max Factor brand of cosmetics sells itself with "the makeup of makeup artists" tagline, while many fitness brands, including Adidas and Yurbud, sell on the back of professional athletes' endorsements with "designed by athletes for athletes" sales copy. And it works, because authority is a powerful persuasion cue.

Fab uses authority to sell. It uses a team of respected design curators to handpick and recommend design ideas to sell on its site. And because Fab makes it easy for customers to share these authoritative design picks with their friends through share buttons on product pages, the sales influence of authority cascades through social networks.

Susceptibility to authority runs deep in human psychology. Want to know how to sell the idea of murder to someone? Use authority. That's what a vivid experiment in 1961 at Yale University showed. In the context of a memory test, an authoritative-looking test organizer asked volunteers to administer increasingly severe electric shocks to each other. Screams of pain notwithstanding, two thirds of the volunteers were willing to administer a deadly 450V shock to their fellow test participants on the mere request of an authority figure. Authority sold them a cruel idea, and they bought it. Fortunately, no one actually died in the memory tests, because those receiving the shocks were actually undercover actors. But it proved the point: most of us will defer or abdicate to an authority figure, whenever we can.[1]

We don't suggest using authority to sell harm, but psychologist Dr. Robert Cialdini does suggest you use it at work to sell your own ideas and your own agenda.[2] Rather than rely on rational or emotional arguments, use the *social argument* that your idea has been endorsed by, or is the same as that of, other recognized experts. And don't forget to establish your own authority, too, by elegantly dropping in your credentials, experience, and knowledge.

SOCIAL MINDSET

By selling with the voice of authority, Fab offers social utility to fans and customers. Through its design curation service, Fab helps customers use their social intelligence—the ability to learn socially from the expertise and experience of others to discover, evaluate, and decide—on great design worth buying. It's a useful social service that, in a design-obsessed world, helps people make great design choices.

But as we saw in the vignette about Dan, Fab also offers a different kind of social utility; it offers social status. Dan not only discovers great design via Fab, but he also reinforces his status, his public image, as a design-minded creative type. Fab's curated design selections allow Dan to stand out from the nondesign crowd and fit into the design crowd. In other words, Fab is selling the ability to both stand out and fit in, which are very useful social benefits. What helps is that Fab is a private members-only club, so its design picks are only known to members, allowing Dan to appear to be a gatekeeper to good taste.

UNLOCKING SOCIAL COMMERCE SALES

Fab uses authority to sell with expert design curators who handpick design ideas for purchase by its private club members. From a commercial mindset this is smart selling; authority is a proven persuasion cue in sales. And it works from a social perspective too—selling with authority allows Fab members to learn from others about great design, and be seen by friends as knowledgeable about what's hot in the world of design. Moreover, by sharing undiscovered design treasures, Fab gives fans word-of-mouth ammunition and motivation to evangelize about how great Fab is. It's smart social selling. The social commerce opportunity is to take Fab's model and adapt it for your business, using expert curation and authoritative recommendations to drive sales.

For example, you might consider inviting recognized experts, celebrities, or even expert users from your customer base to select and showcase a "product of the week" (or month) with an exclusive interview in a special expert or pro area of your store.

Selling with authority lies at the heart of OpenSky, a social commerce start-up that invites online influencers and celebrities to curate and endorse products and take a cut of sales. Martha Stewart is a user, as is TV host and author Zane Lamprey, known as the World Drinking Ambassador. His "expert" product recommendations, which include such items as a beer pong portable tailgate table, hangover cure coffee, and a set of "upside down" beer glasses, certainly have a niche appeal.

Social commerce company Beachmint also draws on the "expert" influence of a number of celebrities—singer/actor Justin Timberlake, actresses Jessica Simpson and Kate Bosworth, stylist Cher Coulter, and celebrities Mary-Kate and Ashley Olsen—to sell socially through its "curated commerce" shopping channels: HomeMint, JewelMint, BeautyMint, StyleMint, and ShoeMint. Likewise, fashion retailer ShoeDazzle takes advantage of the popularity spawned by its high profile cofounder, Kim Kardashian, who uses her unique fashion sense to promote a curated range of shoes, handbags, and jewelry.

But selling with authority doesn't always come from celebrity and professionals. Teenage girls lend their style-smarts to brands by using videos to talk about their latest fashion purchases. Called "haulers," these fashion-savvy young women are posting homemade videos to show off their latest finds. Popular teen hauler Bethany Mota has garnered an audience of over 800,000 subscribers on her YouTube channel, and her videos have been seen over 110 million times.

Even though brands can leverage the authority of well-known celebrities, perhaps even more influential is the authority of a friend who we know, admire, and trust. A number of social shopping sites have emerged to help harness the peer authority:

- Buyosphere allows users to ask questions about product recommendations and receive answers from the community.

- Givvy is a social shopping Facebook app that relies on user-submitted products and human curators to supply its inventory.
- ShopSocially, a site at the forefront of this new genre, gives users the opportunity to ask friends a shopping question or share purchase information with them.

In order to unlock social media sales with authority, consider these starter ideas:

- Discuss how you might adapt the Fab model to what you sell; use the expert curation and a private-shopping club model to offer social utility in the form of smart social discovery and enhanced social status.
- From a commerce mindset, remember that selling with authority is all about using authority as a persuasion cue; how could you embed the borrowed voice of independent authority into your sales copy?
- From a social perspective, using authority means giving your customers expert insights, information, and recommendations that they'll want to share with their friends. Help them do this by using social media to make that information shareable.
- Do you have any products or services that are already favorites with experts or professionals? Consider showcasing and selling these in social media with authority figure endorsements and testimonials.
- Consider setting up a social media store as a pro shop with a small expert-curated range of products, including expert reviews.
- Explore the possibility of working with third-party experts or celebrities, who could front a special product of the week or month.

LIKE AND BE LOVED

I do not want people to be
very agreeable, as it saves me the trouble
of liking them a great deal.

—JANE AUSTEN

CHICAGO BULLS

Like hundreds of millions of others, Ryan uses Facebook to connect and share with the people in his life. The *people*, not the businesses. For Ryan, if it doesn't have a face, it shouldn't really be on Facebook. He tolerates the ads and commercial content on Facebook just as he tolerated the ads of yesteryear on broadcast TV. A necessary evil for a free service. Facebook is a people thing for Ryan, and Ryan uses Facebook to connect with people who matter to him.

Someone who matters to Ryan is Derrick Rose, the NBA basketball superstar from his team, the Chicago Bulls. As an NBA league Most Valuable Player (MVP), Ryan likes Derrick Rose. He likes him a lot. He has the D. Rose jersey, the D. Rose branded Adidas sneakers, and, of course, he follows D. Rose on Facebook, just like 4 million others. He's a fan.

So when Ryan sees a status update on Facebook that the NBA All Star has linked to an online pop-up store selling Bulls branded sports bracelets from Power Balance, Ryan doesn't just notice, he buys.

COMMERCE MINDSET

Commercial wisdom says celebrity sells. And money follows that wisdom; Derrick Rose has a cool $200M+ endorsement deal with Adidas that dwarfs his salary and winnings.[1] But the investment makes sense for Adidas; celebrity endorsement leads to, on average, a 4 percent jump in sales and a corresponding improvement in market share.[2] And shareholders are usually happy too; celebrity endorsements tend to increase stock prices. Of course, there are caveats but bottom line, it's true what they say. Celebrity sells.

For many businesses, social selling through celebrities is simply not an option. But the underlying principle that makes celebrity endorsement work can be harnessed by pretty much any business.

The simple principle is that the human mind works by association. If we associate someone we like with a product, then the positive emotions associated with that person get associated with that product too. The positive emotion "bleeds through" via mental chains of association. This might sounds like psychobabble, but intuitively, we get this. When we associate a product with someone we like, we also tend to like that product too. So it's not that *celebrity* sells, it's that *liking* sells, and it sells by association. Associate your product with people who your customers like, such as their friends, and they'll be more likely to buy. Which is why selling with social media, where friends connect, makes good commercial sense. We like what our friends like.

SOCIAL MINDSET

From a social mindset, the power of "liking by association" becomes even more powerful. Liking products liked by the people we like helps us be liked back. It's a form of flattery that can have affective rewards. When our purchases are influenced by people we like it's usually not because we want to make the *right* decision, but because we want to *be liked*. This social insight has all sorts of commercial implications.

For example, our desire to be liked means we are more likely to buy from our friends, not because we like what they are selling, such as a Tupperware kitchen accessory, but because we want to be liked by them. It's a form of social bonding. I buy this and I am investing in our relationship. Tomorrow you'll like me back by doing something for me. Philosophically speaking, it's "enlightened self-interest of reciprocal altruism" that's at play here. But whatever you call it, this principle powers a lot of social behavior, and it's the reason why so many successful sales pitches include a thinly veiled covert message: buy me and people will like you.

Our desire to be socially liked also means we're more likely to buy from the three kinds of people who we all tend to like and wanted to be liked by: people who are physically attractive; people who are liked by others, i.e. that have high social status; and those who are like ourselves—we tend to like people with whom we identify as similar but better versions of ourselves. So that's why successful sales people tend to be physically attractive and why ads showcase products with people we like or who are like us. (And it's also why, whether you know it or not, your promotion prospects, electability, or likelihood to be found innocent in a court of law are all influenced by how likeable you are, especially in terms of your physical attractiveness.)

UNLOCKING SOCIAL MEDIA SALES

So how can you use the secret power of "liking" to unlock sales with social media? First, understand that it's people, not campaigns, that primarily influence people, especially people who are liked. The social commerce opportunity is to sell down the lines of affinity networks with people-powered sales.

Of course, not every business can sell through A-list or even Z-list celebrities in social media, but if you have the opportunity, use it. If not, don't worry; think instead how you could co-opt your customers to endorse what you sell to their friends. This might range from a simple click of a "Like" button or a post-purchase share on an e-commerce site, to the use of Facebook's "Sponsored

Stories" advertising solution that republishes customer interactions with you into the friends of your customers' newsfeeds.

Whilst the easiest way of selling along the social lines of affinity is to simply install social sharing buttons on your e-commerce site, this is just the tip of the iceberg. Think how you might gently encourage people who buy from you to recommend you to their friends. It might be as simple as offering a pass-it-on voucher or discount. The key thing to remember is that you want customers to influence and be influenced by people they like.

- Social media is a people-first environment. Build your social sales strategy around people selling to people, not corporate or company selling—you'll need to give social selling a human face.
- Consider your options for co-opting celebrities into your social media sales strategy; could they endorse what you are selling, or better still, sell it themselves from their social media page or blog?
- Don't limit yourself to high-profile celebrities. Are there any popular peers that your customers like and admire who could help you sell? Consider working with these influencers.
- Think back to the old-style Tupperware party form of network selling; could you reinvent the model for social media, perhaps with online social sales parties hosted by customers?
- Consider how you could incentivize fans to "soft sell" to friends by sharing offers that would benefit their friends.
- More generally, work to make sales as visible as possible to the friends of your customers, through elective and automatic sharing features in social media.

DRIVE DISCOVERY

In one word, social commerce
is about discovery.

—CHRISTIAN TAYLOR, FOUNDER OF PAYVMENT

GADGET OBSESSION

Justin is a technophile. Discovering new products to add
to his collection is one of Justin's favorite things to do, so
he visits Best Buy two or three times a week to check out
the latest gadgets. His penchant for consumer electronics
is so strong that he spends literally thousands of dollars
per year at the big box store. Justin also loves Facebook,
though he never uses it for shopping. Except this time.

When scanning his news feed, Justin noticed a status update from a friend who had just purchased an iPhone case from an electronics accessories site called Speck.com. Embedded in the update was a link. Justin clicked on it and a small window containing information about the product, along with a "Buy Now" button, opened on his screen.

Having recently purchased a new iPhone, Justin was taken with the quality of the case and decided to purchase it himself. He clicked the button, expecting to be taken to the retailer's website. Much to his surprise, another window opened that gave him the opportunity to securely input credit card information and buy the item without ever leaving Facebook.

It was a serendipitous find and eye-opening for Justin, someone who used to think of Facebook simply as a social network. As a result of that experience, Facebook had become much more: a site not only designed for sharing personal interests, but for discovering new products as well.

COMMERCE MINDSET

One of the reasons shops exist is to encourage shoppers to *discover* new things. Sure, sometimes we know exactly what we want, and where to get it, but often—in fact, most often—we browse without knowing exactly what we're after. Shopping is as much about product discovery as it is about buying. The opportunity for social commerce is to assist not just the "buying" aspect of social media but also the "discovery" component.

So how can social media be deployed to assist product discovery? The simple answer is through social shopping sites that are designed for browsing and sharing as much as they are for searching and transacting. Take a look at sites like Svpply, Fancy, and Polyvore, and you'll see how they differ from Amazon-style marketplaces; they are designed for product discovery and the act of sharing discovered products. As a retailer, you can post your products on these sites and allow new customers to discover what you sell.

You should also deploy social plug-ins on your own website to encourage sharing—Facebook Like buttons, Pinterest Pin buttons, Twitter Tweet buttons, etc. Free and easy to use, you'd need to have a good reason not to put these share buttons next to every product you sell today; share buttons help one person's discovery become a discovery for someone else—and bring in new customers.

But there is a problem: there's just so much other stuff out there competing with your product. How do you cut through the product clutter and social chatter and ensure your product gets noticed?

Marketing maven Seth Godin has the answer, and he calls it a "Purple Cow."[1] A purple cow is something remarkable that stands out from the herd. It's something you'd certainly talk about if you saw it. Godin argues persuasively that the only way to cut through hyperclutter of products and the cacophony of social media is to have something new, unique, and remarkable to sell—like a purple cow. This type of item is something worth discovering because it is something worth talking about.

So how do you know which of your products are purple cows? Well, you know that if it's available on Amazon, it is not a purple cow, because it is not unique. And if it's a very good product, it's also not a purple cow—"very good" is just better sameness as "good." What you want is to be remarkable.

SOCIAL MINDSET

Social media works as an avenue for product discovery because we're likely to pay attention to, and trust, our network of friends and associates, otherwise known as our "social graph." Like Justin, it's not that we're going to Facebook to shop; but if a friend recommends a product, we may have interest in it. At the very least, a friend's recommendation gets our attention, and that is half the battle. Other times, serendipity shines its light on us and we find a product that meets our needs or, even better, isn't something we were looking for but that we can't live without.

Social media drives product discovery not only through our individual social graphs, but through what has come to be known as "interest graphs." That is to say, the people who share the same tastes, interests, and "Likes" as we do. Using interest graphs, social media as a vehicle for commerce can become much more purpose-driven.

Take, for example, Walmart's Facebook gift recommendation app, Shopycat. Shopycat looks at your Facebook friends and analyzes their activity on the social network, including things such as "Likes," shares, and posts, then determines what types of gifts they would most likely want based on those interests. The app then searches through a large product database to find what it surfaces as the right gift. While it may not be my own interests I'm focused on, if I'm out to buy a gift for a friend, the app provides social utility: it solves the problem of what gift to buy.

Not only do we trust the voices of friends and those who share our interest, but we also trust the word of experts. The social shopping site Shop.com uses a network of thousands of "shopping consultants"—i.e., expert shoppers—to help customers discover new products based on their individual needs, which leads to better, more informed purchase decisions. It's not that these customers know these experts personally, or that they are even experts in the truest sense, but because they are called "experts," there is implied trust. The same holds true for the recommendation of a celebrity. If Jessica Simpson (BeachMint) or Kim Kardashian (ShoeDazzle) suggest a certain product, who am I to question their taste? Plus, with the manifold number of options available, combined with a limited time to research such products, letting experts curate items is highly appealing.

Christian Taylor, founder and former CEO of in-Facebook shopping cart app Payvment, says, "Social commerce isn't me asking my mom, but finding others who share similar interests, which leads to discovery." Taylor is so committed to that concept that he says the single purpose of social commerce is discovery. He says:

> Taste [interest] graphs will transform the process of
> product discovery and make it much easier to discover
> and engage around the products you really want.
> The graphs will allow sellers to get their products in
> front of the people most likely to be interested.

Retail has entered a new phase wherein product discovery and purchase decisions are informed by the collective and distributed social intelligence of others. So the secret to social smarts is to drive social discovery through the serendipity of the social graph, the similarity evident between members of the interest graph, and the skill of expert curators.

UNLOCKING SOCIAL SALES

How can you turn social media into social sales using the concept of discovery? Consider the following examples:

- Social shopping sites such as Polyvore, Kaboodle, and Lockerz promote the sharing of products discovered online—thus encouraging social discovery.
- Social shopping apps such as Stickybits and ShopKick promote the sharing of store visits, using scanning technology to encourage store discovery and selection.
- Subscription club sites such as Birchbox, Hoseanna, and Manpacks promote product discovery through, specifically, a surprise in the form of a monthly gift box—thus encouraging social sharing.

Social discovery is about enhancing the retail experience for shoppers, about helping them and their friends discover great new products. Instead of asking how you can sell your product to people, ask how you can *help people discover* your product, something genuinely remarkable and worth talking about.

Social media users are the foundation of today's "recommendation economy" wherein shoppers shop smart using their social intelligence—sharing recommendations to inform product discovery and purchase decisions. This shared discovery and recommendation—via social media—is the secret to unlocking sales with social media.

In a very insightful guest post at Forbes[2], Brian Ficho, CEO of a social commerce site called oBaz.com, said this about discovery:

> [W]hen properly executed, [discovery] is about helping
> consumers find stuff they didn't even know existed. It
> begins by encouraging customers to offer information
> about their interests using a variety of techniques that
> deal in the individual's self-interest, from games and
> metaphors to direct feedback. Moreover, discovery
> is an ongoing process, one that is continually refined
> over time to generate relevance at deeper levels
> regardless of how the person's interests change.

If, as Christian Taylor suggests, the secret to success in social commerce lies with discovery, and, as Brian Ficho indicates, it is an ongoing process, here are some ideas you can use to help shoppers use their social intelligence to promote discovery:

- Add social sharing options to your e-commerce website, such as a Facebook "Like," Tweet This, and Pin It buttons to facilitate sharing activity among customers.
- Create a Facebook app built on users' interest graph to make it easier to discover products based on similar interests and likes.
- Co-opt the use of authority figures—celebrities and tastemakers—to curate and recommend new products to fans and followers.
- Build a recommendation engine that awards points to those who engender trust among community members based on the value of their contributions; those who receive the highest number of ratings receive "expert" or "guru" status.
- Start a subscription club where new products are introduced each month in the form of a surprise gift box; encourage members to share the products via social networks.

BE PURPOSE DRIVEN

What on earth am I here for?

—RICK WARREN

A HALLMARK MOMENT

Michelle was having a "Hallmark Moment." A friend just sent her a sappy card that was meaningful and touching. So meaningful, in fact, that she wanted to share that experience with her friends—on Facebook.

Rather than just submit a status update to her Timeline, Michelle used an app called "Tell Them" that Hallmark had developed just for such occasions. But more than simply sharing her experience, the app allowed her to "make a vow"—to tell someone, perhaps in this case the person who sent the card, something special. It was her way of expressing appreciation, both personally and publicly. If she chose, she could also add the vow to her Timeline, so her friends could see it as well. In addition to submitting her own vow, Michelle could read similar vows created by others—and there were thousands.

At no point during the process was Michelle presented with any special offers or promotional messages from Hallmark. At the end, a discount coupon for greeting cards was offered, but that was it. Michelle didn't take offense at such an action; in fact, she appreciated the service the app provided in giving her the opportunity to share a small, yet serendipitous, moment with others.

COMMERCE MINDSET

This presents us with another secret for successful selling via social commerce: *lead with purpose, not a pitch*. That is, rather than coming out of the gate with a sales message, determine a genuine, authentic purpose that is consistent with your brand, that contributes to the greater good, and promotes the welfare of others. It's a clearly stated, compelling and unique value proposition that will set your brand apart from everyone else; and everything you do in terms of customer engagement stems from it.

In his book, *The Art of the Start*[1], well-known author and entrepreneur Guy Kawasaki said that companies should "make meaning" by letting the motivator be something other than money. Instead, he suggests that we should seek to "make the world a better place."

That's exactly what Nike did with "Nike Plus," "Nike Training Club" and the Nike FuelBand. All are designed to help users stay physically fit by assisting them with workout routines, recommending exercises, and tracking workout activity. Certainly, the brand's ultimate goal is to sell more gear, but Nike realized that in order to do so, it should first "make meaning." With that understanding, the brand crafted this purpose statement: "We exist to help everyone to achieve their athletic potential."

This works for Nike because it positions the company as its customers' "workout partner." To facilitate ease of use, the brand created mobile apps that customers can download to their mobile phones and take with them during their workouts. This purpose-driven approach also works because it is consistent with the brand itself—Nike is all about athleticism. And, it keeps the brand in front of customers at the very time when they need it most: during their workouts.

The same holds true for Hallmark. Its brand promise (purpose) is to act as a conduit for building relationships and creating meaningful connections. This statement defines Hallmark's purpose clearly:

> Life is made up of moments. Both big and small,
> happy and sad. And Hallmark helps you share
> your voice, your thoughts, and your feelings,
> so you can let the people you care about know
> exactly what they mean to you. Through thick and
> thin, the good times and the bad, it's important to
> know that life is a special occasion, and Hallmark
> can help drive the emotional connections that
> make all your relationships meaningful.

Kellogg's is another company that understands the need to put purpose first. Take, for example, its Special K brand, whose purpose is, "We help you get to and stay at the weight you want." Similarly, the big-box electronics retailer Best Buy states its purpose as, "We help you realize your technology dreams."

Rick Warren's popular book *The Purpose Driven Life*[2] begins by asking, "What on earth am I here for?" It's an important question and one that not only individuals should grapple with, but brands as well. Is our purpose merely to shift stock, or is there a greater manifestation?

What brands like Nike, Hallmark, Kellogg's, and Best Buy have come to realize is that *purpose*—especially one that helps people achieve their goals and dreams—is indeed the key to increasing customer loyalty, extending long-term value, and becoming more profitable as a result. And so, one secret to commerce success is to be purpose driven.

SOCIAL MINDSET

If being purpose driven has commercial application, there is no better way to foster it than through social media. Take Hallmark, for example. Its "Tell Them" app captures the very essence of why people use Facebook, and that is to share the events of their lives, big and small, with friends and family.

In his hierarchy of needs theory, psychologist Abraham Maslow states that, beyond the basic physiological and safety needs, comes the need for love and belonging— friendship, family, and sexual intimacy. Beyond that, there exists the need for self-esteem—which comes as we receive the respect of others. Social media has become a conduit though which such needs can be met, at least to some extent. Brands that understand that can create applications that foster such need-meeting activity, just as Hallmark did with its "Tell Them" app.

What we're talking about here is a "do unto others" attitude. It's the same one Dale Carnegie espoused in his classic self-help book *How to Win Friends and Influence People*.[3] In it, Carnegie states that we should focus on the interests of others before our own. That has application for brands, as well as people.

Carnegie also said that the "royal road to a person's heart is to talk about the things he or she treasures most." However, in the case of brands seeking to gain influence using social media, it's not just talking with customers that's most effective but providing platforms that give customers the opportunity to communicate with their friends and others who share similar interests.

It's why brands like Target created the social gifting app "Give with Friends," which allows people to come together to purchase Target gift certificates for others, items like an end-of-the-school-year gift for their children's teacher, or a coworker for his or her birthday, for example. It's also the reason Delta Airlines created its "Away We Go" Facebook app that enables people to plan, share, and book travel together. In both cases, just as with Hallmark, commerce transactions are the ultimate, underlying aim, but a view toward serving others—meeting needs and solving problems—was the idea that guided each application's development.

In other words, it's about providing social utility, which is the act of using social media to solve people's problems socially or solve social problems. Smart brands are using social media to offer "social" value propositions that deliver social utility. And social utility can lead to social sales.

Being purpose driven can also take on an even more altruistic tone. Many brands, for example, have aligned themselves with worthy charities.

In *Cause Marketing Through Social Media*[4], authors Kate Olsen and Geoff Livingston cite the case of Tyson Foods and its Hunger Relief program. For the past several years, the company has focused on adding value to the community of those engaged in the fight against hunger by utilizing in-kind donations and social media resources such as its own Hunger Relief site, Twitter account, Facebook page, Flickr group, and YouTube channel to create awareness of hunger and those involved in the issue.

When asked what he thought the biggest takeaways from Tyson Foods Hunger Relief effort were, Ed Nicholson, Director of Community and Public Relations, Tyson Foods, Inc., said, "Shine the spotlight on the cause and what others are doing, rather than yourself. It will generally reflect favorably back on you. Pound-for-pound, authentic engagement trumps cash."

Even so, there is a commercial pay-off for companies that, like Tyson, seek to "make meaning" with charitable connections. A study on cause marketing by public relations firm Cone Communications[5] found that price and quality being equal, most consumers—80 percent—will buy cause-related products over those that don't have a charitable tie-in.

Each of these examples represent social media best practices that can lead to increased brand awareness, greater customer loyalty and even advocacy. Do good, lead with an authentic purpose that helps others, and accrue the benefits that will doubtless come your way. It may be hard for bottom-liners, whose only goal is to make a profit to hear, but it's the way that social media works. Get used to it and get on with driving sales by being purpose driven.

UNLOCKING SOCIAL SALES

So what does all this mean for social commerce? Simple, if you want to shift stock with social media start with a purpose that puts the needs and interests of your customers first. Your product should be featured, but it's the support role, not the leading role.

Michelle's experience with Hallmark's Tell Them app is the perfect case in point. Only at the end of the process, after her making a vow, was she presented with a product-related offering. And she didn't mind because Hallmark had provided her with a way to communicate a moment that she found meaningful and share it with others without inserting itself along the way. The approach paid off because, in Michelle's case, she chose to take advantage of the offer.

In this chapter, you've read several catch phrases—be purpose driven, make meaning, and provide social utility. But it all starts by drafting a genuine, authentic purpose—a unique value proposition consistent with your brand that focuses on meeting the needs and solving the problems of others. Social commerce works—and works best—when brands have this as their singular goal. Be purpose driven. That's the secret.

- Get to know your customer; it's imperative to know and understand the needs and problems of your customer before you can figure out ways to address them.
- Determine your brand's unique value proposition and apply that toward creating a genuine purpose that has as its aim helping people.
- Make your product a secondary focus; put the needs and problems of your customer first.

- Provide social utility by building applications or features that help people solve problems socially or solve social problems.
- Is there a charitable tie-in that would position your brand as altruistic? If so, make sure it's consistent with your brand's value proposition.

DELIVER ZMOTS

The secret to marketing success
is no secret at all: Word of mouth
is all that matters.

—SETH GODIN

MARLEY

Zoe has just seen *Marley*, the 2012 movie directed by
Kevin Macdonald (*State of Play*, *The Last King of Scotland*,
and *Touching the Void*) documenting the life story of musi-
cian, revolutionary, and legend, Bob Marley. Zoe went to
see *Marley* not in a movie theater but on Facebook. *Marley*
was the first movie to be released simultaneously on the
movie's Facebook page and in traditional theaters.

Interestingly, Zoe heard about Marley in a rather traditional way, through traditional advertising: specifically, posters on the subway. But that wasn't why she decided to see the movie. The reason she saw it was because she received a text message from a friend who had just see the movie and loved it. That recommendation was what Google[1] has dubbed Zoe's "Zero Moment of Truth" (a "ZMOT" for short, pronounced *zee-mot*)—a shared experience that validated the call to action from the billboard ad.

The Zero Moment of Truth is simply a shared "truth" (somebody's subjective experience) that influences a purchase decision. It's like an experiential epiphany: you suddenly "get" that you need to buy something based on someone else's experience. And it's based on the simple insight that adding creditability to advertising messages with people's "true" experience results in effective influence. TRUTH + ADVERTISING = SALES.

COMMERCE MINDSET

The ZMOT idea is not new. (A cynic might say it's just Google's attempt to rebrand a very old concept—word of mouth—and our ability to learn from it.) Businesses have been selling with ZMOTs ever since they began used customer testimonials like, "Don't take our word for it" and "See what our customers say." The ZMOT is just a customer testimonial rebranded for the social media age.

But the ZMOT concept is useful because it situates experiences shared by word of mouth within the powerful "Moments of Truth" model of the customer journey that is used by one of the planet's biggest marketers: Procter & Gamble.

Back in the early 2000s, P&G made the case for in-store sensory marketing, revealing that some 70 percent of all purchase decisions are made in-store. They dubbed the moment when a customer first sees a product on the shelf, a first moment of truth: the moment where advertising hype gives way to true first-hand sensory experience. And because we are experiential creatures—heavily influenced by our senses and emotions—P&G suggested these first 3–7 seconds when a shopper encounters a product on a store shelf are absolutely critical in turning browsers into buyers. They changed their marketing spend accordingly, spending less on traditional advertising, and more on sensory marketing, such as in-store sampling. If the first moment of truth turns browsers into buyers, the second experiential moment of truth happens when the buyers actually use the product themselves, and turns "trial-ers" into "loyals." For some P&G brands, the second moment of truth—the proof of the pudding—is quite literally in the eating.

What Google has done with the ZMOT concept is to turn the "Moments of Truth" journey from a path into a viral loop. A first moment of truth (experiencing the product in-store) leads to a second moment of truth (experiencing the product oneself). But this second moment of truth, when it is shared with others, can then be *somebody else's* initial moment of truth—before they see it on sale. This shared experience is the Zero Moment of Truth for the person to whom it's shared.

From a Moments-of-Truth perspective, the key to unlocking sales with social media is to use social media to provide customers with the shared moments of truth, personal experiences with the products you are selling. Selling with ZMOT experiences means adding the credibility of real customer experiences to your sales and marketing messages.

SOCIAL MINDSET

The secret to unlocking sales with social media is to use social media as a ZMOT platform where customers share and learn from each other's experiences—in the form of shared comments, content, ratings, reviews, or recommendations. And customers value ZMOTs—both sharing them and learning from them. Indeed, ZMOTs are "customer magnets," as a study by Sociable Labs reveals:[2]

- 56 percent of online shoppers have clicked on "Like" buttons related to products.
- 38 percent of online shoppers have shared comments with friends about products they have purchased.
- 62 percent of online shoppers have read product comments shared by their friends on Facebook.
- 75 percent of the people who read these comments have clicked on the product image, linking them to the retailer's site.
- 53 percent of those who went to the retailer's site have purchased the product when they got there.
- This "Share-to-Purchase" funnel has resulted in 25 percent of all online shoppers purchasing a product via social sharing.
- 38 percent of online shoppers are sharing product comments with friends on Facebook.
- 62 percent of online shoppers are reading product comments shared by their friends on Facebook.
- Reading comments on Facebook causes 47 percent of all shoppers to click over from these comments and visit retailer sites.
- Once they click over to a retailer, 25 percent of all shoppers purchase on those sites.
- 81 percent of these "Social Buyers" are "Social Sharers," too, turning the share-to-purchase-funnel into a viral sales loop.

UNLOCKING SOCIAL SALES

Given that consumers are using social media to interrupt the traditional purchase funnel by doing product research and that they are relying on the influence of friends (including those on social networks), along with consumer reviews and expert opinions, the secret to unlocking social sales is to provide ZMOT opportunities that enable potential customers to interact with your brand and products.

What does ZMOT mean for you and your business? Two things:

1. If the ZMOT acts as first reality check in the consumer journey, then it is a gatekeeper and agenda-setter for customer acquisition. 25 percent of Dell's new customers are the result of a positive ZMOT. That means your advertising should line up with the product experience—since a shared experience is what links advertising to personal experience. So, as we like to say, when crafting your sales and marketing strategy, "start with the smile" of product experience and work backwards.

2. In cases where the ZMOT acts as first reality check in the consumer journey, then the principal role of social media in commerce and marketing is "social utility"—helping people shop smarter with their social intelligence and profit from social situations. In other words, don't offer campaigns; offer social utility. Your social strategy should be about using social media to help people discover and decide smarter.

With the above in mind, the two areas where social media provides social utility are customer acquisition and loyalty. Customer acquisition and loyalty are two distinct activities, of course, but at the top of the customer loyalty ladder lays advocacy, and advocacy creates a "viral loop" that transforms loyal customers into new customer acquisition machines—a volunteer sales force. Advocacy acts as a ZMOT for new customers, helping them discover and decide what to buy.

In his e-book on the ZMOT, author Jim Lecinski quotes Kim Kadlec, worldwide vice president of Johnson & Johnson's Global Marketing Group, who said:

> We're entering an era of reciprocity. We now have to engage people in a way that's useful or helpful to their lives. The consumer is looking to satisfy their needs, and we have to be there to help them with that. To put it another way: How can we exchange value instead of just sending a message?

How can your company use social media to create Zero Moments of Truth? Here are some ideas:

- Create a blog to provide product information and expert advice, and optimize the blog so that it appeals to search engines.
- Incorporate rating and review software as a way to educate customers and keep on your site rather than going elsewhere to do product research.
- Use Facebook "Like," Tweet This, Pin It, and Google +1 buttons on product pages to facilitate social sharing, so that one person's ZMOT becomes another's ZMOT.
- Set up a YouTube channel to promote behind-the-scenes videos, customer testimonials, instructional how-to videos, and TV commercials; people love video and, from a search marketing perspective, YouTube is the second largest search engine owned by the largest, Google, so it makes sense to have a presence there.

- Are you getting the most benefit from your Facebook page? Facebook has become the epicenter for almost every type of social commerce activity, so not only can you use it to promote f-commerce campaigns, but you can also use it to engage with customers and encourage viral sharing.
- Create a branded online community to bring customers in-house where your brand and products are put front and center without the distractions found on social networks.
- How can you use Pinterest? Think in terms of providing content that inspires and informs and that is based on customer's interests.
- Last but not least, think of the many ways you can use Twitter, from product promotion to CRM to new customer acquisition.

FLIP THE FUNNEL

Give your fans the power
to speak up.

—SETH GODIN

GIFFGAFF

Alan works for Giffgaff, a British pay-as-you-go mobile
network. Actually, you could say he runs the company.
Yet he doesn't actually *work* for Giffgaff; Alan is not an
employee in the traditional sense, but he, along with
Giffgaff's thousands of other customers, have an ownership stake, thanks to a philosophy upon which the
company is based: "mutuality."

The company's name comes from an old Scottish word, *giffgaff*, which means "mutual giving." That idea serves as the philosophical framework upon which Giffgaff is built. Even its tagline—"the mobile network run by you"—tells the story. There is a real sense of partnership—mutuality—that exists between the company and its customers, who are called "giffgaffers," and Alan is proud to stake an ownership claim.

Giffgaff hands over the reins to its customers in several ways. For example, Alan is a part of the customer service department, answering questions through the online community forums. He works in R&D, providing product development ideas. He's even joined the sales force, recruiting several of his Facebook friends into the fold. But there is more to this arrangement than just love for the brand; Giffgaff rewards Alan with money, which he can apply toward his phone bill.

It's a pretty sweet deal for both parties. Giffgaff saves on operating costs and Alan saves on his phone bill. Even more important, the company's willingness to entrust its customers with the management of critical business functions like customer service leads to benefits that are more intrinsic and less tangible—a sense of partnership, ownership, and mutual respect.

COMMERCE MINDSET

Giffgaff's model provides us with another secret to selling: empower your customers by giving up, or ceding, a degree of control to them. When you empower people, you create enthusiastic stakeholders more willing to buy more, for more, for longer and, critically—recommend more. And while ceding power to customers is likely to strike fear in the heart of any brand manager, marketing team, or advertising agency, the polarity shift that has taken place in the way we communicate—from top-down to bottom-up—means it's a necessary step that can pay big dividends. To make the idea a bit more palatable, let me use another term popularized by two bestselling authors Seth Godin and Joseph Jaffe: you need to "flip the funnel."

Joseph Jaffe's book *Flip the Funnel* is highly recommended as one of the best books on social media and selling. Here it is in a nutshell. You've most likely heard of the traditional sales funnel and the AIDA model: first, make your audience *Aware* of what you are selling; then, create *Interest*; next, *Desire*; and, finally, move them to *Action* as they buy your product. Well, Jaffe advocates "flipping the funnel" and *starting* with the sale; that is, starting with customers you already have. First, *Acknowledge* your customers; next, engage them in *Dialogue*; then, *Incentivize* further action; and, finally, *Activate* recommendation and additional purchases.

Flipping the funnel makes sound commercial sense. Just ask yourself: what proportion of your business comes from existing customers vs. new customers? Now compare this to your sales and marketing spend—how much is spent on existing customers vs. new customers? Is there a mismatch? Ask your new customers how many came to you via marketing messages, and how many came via word of mouth. There's probably a mismatch there, too, between what you spend on advocacy activation vs. old-style AIDA selling.

In *Flip the Funnel*, Jaffe reveals that the secret to unlocking sales is to deliver experiences to existing customers that are worth recommending. Think about Apple and its in-store Genius Bars. They are genius not only because they get people into the store with a free offer (how many times have you ever left an Apple store without buying something?), but they also enhance the value proposition and create another reason to recommend. American Express has its innovative Open Forum, a forum for B2B customers to help each other with expert commentary and advice. Or think of Amazon, eschewing advertising and investing instead in smart recommendation-building customer experiences, such as its "free" fast shipping and returns service, Amazon Prime.

The message is simple but commercially smart: *flip the funnel and make customer retention your new acquisition strategy.* In other words, focus your sales and marketing investment on delivering remarkable experiences worth recommending. That is the secret to sustainable growth. Whether we like it or not, the truth is that the funnel has flipped, and smart brands have figured out ways to leverage that megaphone effect to their commercial advantage.

It's why companies like Dell and Starbucks have created sites—Ideastorm and MyStarbucksIdea, respectively—for crowdsourcing consumer ideas on product features and ways to improve customer experience. By listening and acting, they build products tailored to the needs and wants of the consumer and create enthusiastic advocates. This business ethic of "connect and collaborate" rather than "command and control" can be applied not only to innovation but marketing, too. For example, in 2007, confectioner Cadbury invited consumers to take its popular Gorilla television commercial, remix it and distribute their creations on YouTube. A great creative ad became "our ad"—driving affinity, loyalty, and funnel-flipping advocacy.

From a commerce standpoint, flipping the funnel like this makes sense for three reasons: first, it focuses investment on where your revenue actually comes from, your existing customers; second, it drives customer loyalty—propensity to repurchase—a key driver of revenue; and third, it activates advocacy, another key driver of revenue. Therefore, commercially, it pays to flip the funnel.

SOCIAL MINDSET

Flipping the funnel certainly has implications where social media is concerned. What bigger megaphone exists today than social networks like Facebook and Twitter, and what better way to turn customers into a sales force than by leveraging the social technologies?

In his e-book *Flipping the Funnel*, author and marketing guru Seth Godin puts it this way: "Turn strangers into friends, friends into customers, and customers into salespeople." When it comes to social media, we call this team of salespeople "friends," "fans," and "followers." Anything you can do to incite social sharing and get people talking about you is worth the effort.

Of course, that's fine and dandy when fans and followers say nice things about the brand. But how about when they don't? Many brands fear the notion of putting themselves in a position to be criticized in an open forum.

One brand willing to not only tolerate but embrace negative sentiment is Marmite, a food spread made from yeast extract. Due to its rather distinctive (some would say "peculiar") taste, the product has a reputation for being either loved or hated. For years, the company has taken that reputation and used it to their advantage in a clever marketing campaign that thrives via social media. Visit the Marmite website and you are introduced to a graphic containing the brand's logo. To the left of the logo is a heart-shaped image overlaid with the words, "I'm a lover." To the right is another image with the words, "I'm a hater." Click the image on the left and you are taken to a page where you can join a fan club, purchase Marmite products, and visit the Marmite "Love" Facebook Page.

The interesting thing is you get similar results when clicking the "I'm a hater" image: you can join the Marmite Hater fan club and visit a Facebook page just for haters where you will read posts like, "I'd rather _____ than eat Marmite," which received 434 comments.

Most brands are happy to flip the funnel and give the megaphone to the lovers who will speak with adoration, but very few would give equal time and space to those who speak negatively. Yet, this tongue-in-cheek approach has worked well for Marmite and generated an even greater degree of customer loyalty than it already had. (In the UK Marmite is a household name.) And research consistently shows that customer feedback on websites—whether positive or negative—boosts sales; negative feedback is OK because it adds credibility and believability to a stream of feedback.[1]

Still, the social focus of your flip-the-funnel strategy should be to activate advocacy and facilitate sharing. Brands such as Apple, Nike, Withings, and Intuit all integrate social media into their products, inviting people to share happy moments, like finishing your tax return, losing weight, or completing a run. They make products that are social by design. The secret to unlocking sales with social media is to embed sharing into the product experience.

UNLOCKING SOCIAL SALES

Social media has given consumers a megaphone through which to broadcast their ideas and opinions about brands and products. And they are taking full advantage. Can retailers, in turn, take advantage of this flipping of the funnel and partner with consumers using social commerce to produce revenue? You bet!

Tennis shoe manufacturer Converse started a campaign called "Create" that turns its customers into designers and quasi-retailers. For $75, shoppers can have a pair of their very own, personally designed shoes that they can also sell to friends and other shoppers.

Clothing and home goods site Cut on Your Bias uses crowdsourcing and permits consumers to interact on preproduction decisions with designers, creating opportunities for virtual collaboration between consumer and designer.

Though not sponsored by retailers, Tug of Store is a real-time "tug of war" online game that allows visitors to rate products as "crap" or "cool." Products appear in the game through an API feed from Svpply, and those that are rated as "cool" can be purchased from participating stores.

This flipping the funnel concept puts consumers in charge of their own destinies. It solves the problem of making purchase decisions by enabling them to rely on the opinions and choices of others. It also solves a social problem—fitting in—by making them one member of a contingent of others (giffgaffers, for example) who share an interest in the brand.

By turning consumers into designers, cocreators, and retailers, brands increase their chances that the products developed will do a better job of meeting the demands of the marketplace. And they stand a solid chance of keeping those same customers long-term, thereby increasing loyalty and advocacy. The secret to successful social commerce is to flip the funnel and turn retention into your customer acquisition strategy.

- Align your sales and marketing costs to your revenue: if 70 percent of revenue comes from existing customers, your budget should reflect this.
- Ask your customers what prompted them to come to you in the first place. If 50 percent came to you by recommendation, then half of your sales and marketing effort should be invested in stimulating recommendations.
- Add social plug-ins to your site to enable customers to share freely.
- Whenever you run an event, think about how you could use it to bring existing customers together with prospects, and let the power of recommendation do its magic.
- Can you take the cue from Apple and Nike and build social sharing actually into your product or service—either electronically, with smart social media connectivity, or "old school," by bringing people together at marketing events?
- Create video content that you encourage fans and followers to remix and make their own, then share with friends.
- Start a brand ambassador program and reward enthusiastic fans with loyalty points, exclusive products, and early access to company news in exchange for social sharing.
- How about asking a select group of loyal customers to serve on a customer advisory board? Seek their advice on products, R&D, customer service practices, and take their input seriously.
- Provide crowdsourcing opportunities that give customers the ability to suggest new features and even new products.

- Incorporate a ratings and review system in your e-commerce website; provide points toward purchase discounts in exchange for participation.
- Turn customers into a massive salesforce; incentivize recruitment and sales activity with special offers, discounts, and rebates.
- Think about other ways you can encourage customers to talk about and extend your brand's message with their friends on social networks.

INTEREST PAYS

Passion is energy. Feel the power
that comes from focusing
on what excites you.
—OPRAH WINFREY

INTEREST IN PINTEREST

Jennifer has just spotted a dress that she knows her young daughter Alyssa will just love. It's a pink, flowery, and exceptionally girly dress from Halabaloo. Jennifer spotted the dress on Pinterest, the popular image-sharing and scrapbooking site organized around themed online "pinboards" of images clipped from the web and "pinned" according to interest area.

Jennifer is a dedicated follower of kids' fashion and uses Pinterest to create and share online scrapbooks of fashion finds for Alyssa. She pins the Hulabaloo dress to her party clothes pinboard, allowing it to be seen and then "repinned" on other users' Pinterest pinboards if they like the dress too. In doing this, Jennifer is also participating in a novel sales campaign from leading e-commerce fashion retailer, Gilt. If the Hulabaloo dress gets repinned on 50 different Pinterest pinboards, it goes on sale on Gilt for $28, or 77 percent off the full retail price. Click on the dress image when the deal is live, and it will take you to the Gilt product page where you can make a purchase.

The Gilt Kids "Pin It to Unlock" sales promotion is a new take on group buying: rather than require a minimum number of people to commit to buying a product in order to unlock a deal, all that is required is a minimum number of users to repin a product image in order to unlock a deal. Within hours, the Gilt deal is live. It's smart because it uses the power of images to sell—a picture is worth a thousand words—combined with people's personal interests.

COMMERCE MINDSET

The secret to unlocking sales is to focus on people's interests and passions. It's an old but effective sales technique: customize the sales pitch to people's personal interests in order to make the product appear more relevant and compelling. Pinterest uses people's interests, energies, and passions to sell.

Although Pinterest could be considered a social network, it doesn't rely on the "social graph"—the network of personal connections—as the impetus for the activity that takes place on the site. Instead, it puts emphasis on what is referred to as the "interest graph": the network of shared interests. Even though sites like Pinterest have brought the interest graph to our attention, interest-oriented marketing has been around for years, and there is no better example of this approach in action than in the legendary rock band the Grateful Dead.

In their popular book *Marketing Lessons from the Grateful Dead,*[1] authors David Meerman Scott and Brian Halligan discuss how, almost from the band's founding in 1967, fans of the Grateful Dead—"Deadheads" as they came to be called—saw themselves as something more than lovers of the band's music. They felt as if they were members of a "spiritual community," and thousands of them followed the band literally everywhere they went. The Grateful Dead made sure its marketing efforts appealed to that mindset.

A notice tucked inside the 1971 album *Skull and Roses* invited fans to join a mailing list, which promised to keep them informed of upcoming concerts and other news. But, according to Scott and Halligan, the newsletter functioned more like a pre-Internet social network where fans could "opt-in, connect with each other at shows, share common interests, be informed of upcoming events, and feel like they were part of a community."

But shared-interest marketing extends well beyond pinboards and rock bands. It is also deeply ingrained into the established business community. Industry-related trade expos are but one example. Potential buyers come together around a shared interest, and if your company's products or services meet their needs, you've got a new buyer. Not only that, but local Chambers of Commerce have what they refer to as Shared Interest Groups (SIGs), where members with similar interests meet regularly to discuss trends, issues, and ideas.

From a commerce perspective, selling through people's interests and passions is smart. Identify communities of interest rather than demographics, and sell with offers adapted to them and relevant to their passions. This simply makes for an easier sell.

SOCIAL MINDSET

People talk about their passions and interests on social networks, so it makes sense to sell by appealing to people's passions. Appeal to what people love and they will talk and share—and bring in new customers. Remember, from a social mindset, your existing customers are your means to acquire new customers; you want them to come back for more and bring their friends. And the simplest way of doing this is to sell to people already passionate about the area you are selling in. If you delight enthusiasts, you turn their enthusiasm into recommendations and referrals.

In his article, "So What Comes After Social Commerce?"[2] Om Malik, the founder of technology news site GigaOm, suggests that the interest graph more closely resembles Twitter than Facebook. He says, "Just as you can follow someone . . . without being his friend, you can have an asymmetrical relationship with someone who has similar musical interests or taste in watches."

To put it another way, if the social graph is a "sociogram" that maps people and their relationships, an interest graph is an "infogram" that maps people and their interests. The difference is more significant than meets the eye. Just because my Facebook friend is wild about *foie gras,* for example, doesn't mean that I also have a penchant for goose liver paté. On the other hand, even though I may not know a person based on a social connection, a shared interest binds us together in certain ways. As such, selling to people who have similar interests carries a greater value proposition than selling to those who don't, even though they may be socially connected.

However, selling through peoples' *interests* does not necessarily always trump selling through people's *connections.* The sweet spot is *where the interest graph and the social graph intersect*: with people who know each other *and* share each others' passions. Here, information spreads without friction through network of affinity, powered by shared passion. And with the ability to connect in social media with experts, celebrities, and public figures who share or embody your passion, the interest graph effectively extends the social graph. What this means for social commerce is that you should consider selling through experts, celebrities, and public figures, as well as through friends and family.

UNLOCKING SOCIAL SALES

The secret to unlocking social commerce sales is to utilize social technologies and platforms in ways that tie into people's interests and passions. An outstanding example of how to do this is a campaign using Pinterest run by online retailer Land's End. Called "Pin It to Win It," the brand asked followers to browse its LandsEndCanvas .com website and pin their favorite items to Pinterest pinboards for a chance to win gift cards valued at $250. Land's End promoted the contest on Facebook and highlighted winning pinboards there, as well. In this instance, the area of shared interest was not just the clothes, but the brand itself.

The approach used by Land's End was very campaign-specific, but that doesn't always have to be the case. Tying Twitter hashtags to discounts, seasonal promotions, or special events is another way for this to work. Luxury automaker Jaguar promoted its global "Alive" initiative on Twitter by creating a "#FeelAlive" hashtag and advertised it using Twitter Promoted Tweets to amplify the message.

Om Malik's belief is that the formula "interest graph + commerce = transactions" may be more powerful than "social graph + commerce = transactions." Where social commerce is concerned, the business opportunity is to generate value discovery, validation, recommendation— for and from people with shared *interests* rather than shared contacts.

Furthermore, if the future of social commerce lies with the interest graph, then there will be opportunities for using tried and tested social commerce tools, notably group-buy, social network stores, and curated reviews, within specific industry verticals (or "interest verticals"). Think in terms of specialist group-buy sites for business areas, sports, hobbies, and so on.

Indeed, as social media expands further and becomes more fragmented, it is the interest graph that should guide you as a retailer or marketer, rather than the social graph. After all, we rarely buy anything simply because some friends we knew from school bought it, too, but the recommendation from people who are passionate about a category implies authority and a depth of knowledge, so we are more open to influence.

This brings us to a rather arcane sounding but important debate about how influence works in social media; the so-called "homophily vs. contagion" debate. In the early days of social media it was widely thought that behavior, such as buying your product, spreads through social network through a process of personal influence (in techno-jargon, "social contagion"): one customer influences another. But newer research shows that personal influence may be less important than we originally thought. What seems to happen is that people gravitate to others who share their interests, so you get clusters of people doing and buying similar things not because they influence each other but because they share similar interests. This is called "homophily," which is just more techno-jargon for "birds of a feather flock together." If this is the case, then the role of social media and shopping may be less about friends influencing friends and more about making *new* friends based on similar interests. These new friends can then wield collective buying power by getting together and buying with bulk discounts. Think Sam's Club and Costco reinvented, where buying clubs exist for people with shared passions. That is the future of social commerce, and it's the big commercial opportunity for you as a business.

To get started on unlocking sales with the interest graph, here are some ideas for how you can use Pinterest, Twitter, and other social networks to harness the power of shared passions:

- Run a "Pinterest Lottery" where you ask users to "repin" numbered images you have posted. Each week, select an image at random and enter those who have repinned it into a drawing for a special prize.
- Run a Pinterest promotion, where prices vary based on the number of times a product image is repinned.
- Think how you might publish your product catalog on Pinterest in a series of curated and themed boards.
- Ask Pinterest members to pin their favorite product images from your e-commerce website for a chance to win the product itself or gift cards for use on the site.

- Make it as easy for visitors to your site to pin products; Pinterest offers a "Pin it" button that can be placed on every product detail page.
- Repin images from Pinterest members on your company page; this serves to provide inspiration, attract attention, and support social sharing. In turn, this could lead to interest being shown in the product images you've posted, and then to the products themselves.
- Not a product company? Pinterest doesn't have to be just about products; it can be about business services, as well. Think reports, infographics, images associated with blog posts, and so on.
- Consider the influence of tastemakers; trust in experts could yield more fruitful results than those of friends and other users.
- Use Twitter hashtags to draw attention to product promotions, special events, and contests; encourage Tweeters to use the hashtag in their Tweets.
- Make your customer's lifestyle and taste graph top priority. Pinterest provides a canvas—indeed, a tabula rasa—for creative expression; this blank canvas demands that brands go beyond a product-push mentality and adopt a social mindset that puts the interests of consumers first.
- Think in terms of social utility; provide a social service that helps people find social solutions to problems or that solves social problems. Think of sites like Pinterest as a tool to help people discover, evaluate, and decide socially based on their shared experience.

SELL SHOVELS

The ones who make the money are
the men who sell the shovels.

—SAMUEL BRANNAN

CANDLETINI

Jan makes candles. Not just any candle, mind you, but
candles that look and smell like martinis. You know, the
"fashionable" and trendy kind—chocolatini, lemon drop,
appletini, and more. She refers to her creations as "can-
dletinis." And she sells them exclusively on the leading
online arts and crafts marketplace Etsy, through which
an estimated $1 billion in sales are conducted every year.[1]

Because most of Etsy's customers are women, it is the ideal environment in which to showcase her products. Also, Jan doesn't have to compete against the broad range of categories found on sites like eBay and Amazon. Etsy limits sellers to one of three categories: crafters, artists, or collectors. The site allows people to sell their handmade creations, vintage goods, and crafting supplies, which gives it a boutique feel well suited to the type of product Jan is selling.

Due to the transparency invoked by the social nature of the site, Jan can get to know her buyers on a more personal level. She can see their faces, know their names, and read their profiles, which gives her the sense that she belongs to a community. Best of all, Etsy is less complicated and less expensive to use than sites like eBay. For all these reasons, Etsy has proven to be a boon to Jan's small, home-based business.

COMMERCE MINDSET

For businesses like Jan's, this marketplace approach to selling is perfect. Her experience, along with those of the more than 800,000 sellers who call Etsy home, reveals the secret that is the focus of this chapter: one way to be successful in selling is to provide a marketplace where buyers and sellers come together to exchange goods and services.

Many modern-day companies have adopted this approach, but such marketplaces existed even in ancient times. One of the earliest could be found in Greece, dating as far back as the 10th century BC. Central to every Greek city and town was the *agora*², a marketplace and central gathering place for the community. Platforms, altars, and statues of gods, sportsmen, and political figures could be found there. And so could commerce.

In the open area of the agora, vendors set up their shaded tables and sold such items as meat, fish, fruits, and vegetables, along with cheeses, eggs, honey, wine, olive oil, and animals (such as donkeys, horses, and hens). Fresh meat and fish were displayed on marble slabs that kept the food cool. "Fast food" was even sold to hungry shoppers. Craftsmen had stalls, shops, or workshops in or nearby where they sold their goods or took orders. Bankers also conducted business here. In the shady parts of the agora, family and friends could meet for a chat, while businesspeople could make deals. Citizens could join in, or listen to, discussions about community and politics, and they may even have watched musical and theatrical entertainment. A similar environment thrived in Roman forums and Middle Eastern *souks*. Busy and bustling, all were central gathering places that provided a vital hub for the community.

By today's standards, the most obvious translation of this concept may be shopping malls. More grass-roots versions are flea markets, swap meets, or street fairs. Such marketplaces exist online as well, and with much more sophistication. DHgate.com, a B2B and B2C e-commerce marketplace, provides an online trade plat-form where Chinese sellers can connect to buyers from around the globe, including the United States, Europe, Australia, and Asia—over 230 countries in all. The site represents more than 100,000 Chinese sellers offering products in hundreds of categories ranging from agri-cultural supplies to wedding party favors. The site works because it eases the pain of product discovery, provides an experienced customer support team, and is a secure environment in which to transact business. It shrinks an otherwise unwieldy global marketplace into one that's manageable, trusted, and safe.

Another company, 99Designs, is a marketplace that matches those in need of logo and web design with freelance designers. The site works because designers bid on projects, and even create concepts based on project requirements submitted by the buyer. Presented with a number of designs, the buyer then selects the winning bid. 99Designs is a win/win for both buyer and seller. It gives the buyer many affordable options from which to choose, and supplies the designer with many projects upon which to bid.

But this marketplace approach to selling isn't restricted to providing spaces to bring buyers and sellers together. A variation is to provide the tools necessary to help people sell.

During the 1800's California Gold Rush, a San Francisco merchant named Samuel Brannan[3] was credited as one of the chief publicists of the gold rush and also one of its first millionaires. He did not make his fortune digging for gold, however, but for supplying the shovels needed to do so. In fact, the story goes that Brannan bought up every shovel in the city, then grabbed a handful of gold dust and ran through the streets shouting, "There's gold in the American River! There's gold! There's gold!" Whether the story is true or not, it still makes a point about the secret of successful selling: don't dig for gold; sell the shovels.

Fast-forward to today. Intel doesn't make computers but the chips that make them work. Oil field services company Baker Hughes doesn't drill for oil but manufactures the equipment needed by those that do. Similarly, WordPress doesn't build websites but provides the software for designers to use. In each case, this variation on the marketplace theme succeeds due to its focus on furnishing tools essential to meet the needs of the seller. In summary, one secret to successful selling is to create a marketplace that brings buyers and sellers together; the other is to provide the tools to help others sell.

SOCIAL MINDSET

Social media is a "gold mine" for this marketplace mentality because, through social media, the power of one's social networks can be harnessed for product discovery and purchase, all within the confines of community-based interactions. Many companies have tapped into this secret and created such marketplaces. One such example the is T-shirt maker Threadless.com.

As a fashion brand operating in the highly competitive and largely commoditized T-shirt market, Threadless has an enviable reputation; it sells out of every line it produces. However, rather than sell its own T-shirts designs, Threadless is a curated social marketplace that connects T-shirt designers with their customers through talent contests.

The mechanism is simple and elegant: the 600,000+ regular site visitors to Threadless are always presented with three options: become a contestant on the site's latest T-shirt design contest and submit a design, become a member of the contest jury and vote on a design, or be a customer— and buy one of the previous winning designs. Every few days, Threadless takes the most popular of newly submitted designs, puts them into production, and sells them on the site. Winning contestants receive a $2,500 prize in return for commercial rights, and they get their name put on the T-shirt label. Winning designs always sell out.

Another example is Apple and the money it makes from Apple iTunes and the App store/iBookstore. Apple is curating a giant social marketplace—not actually producing anything, but connecting buyers with sellers and adding value with social media by helping people buy and sell smarter. With its iTunes marketplace, Apple is more like an online impresario or talent spotter than a retailer, connecting artists with their markets—and pulling in a healthy commission on sales.

This begs a question: could social marketplaces curated by big brands be the future of big business social commerce? Consumer goods giant Nestlé is experimenting with the idea. In 2011 the company joined the social commerce movement, launching an innovative new social marketplace called Nestlé Marktplatz, which allows consumers to discover, shop, and share 72 Nestlé brands.

Piloted in Germany, this direct-to-consumer marketplace showcases Nestlé's extended brand range, giving German customers exclusive access to new yet-to-be commercialized products, and products not otherwise commercialized in Germany (such as Baci Perugina chocolate pralines from Italy and extra-spicy Maggi chilli sauce from Malaysia).

Significantly, Nestlé engages Marktplaz customers as brand advisors—inviting ideas and suggestions for new products, packaging, and usage occasions. In other words, the marketplace is not only a forum for buying and selling, it's also a forum for conversations between customers—who can rate, comment, seek advice, and share ideas with each other—and a forum designed to foster conversations between the brand and its customers.

Integrating this kind of "empowered involvement" is a smart move for Nestlé, not only because it will help generate useful consumer insight, turning the marketplace into a live learning lab, but it will also drive loyalty and advocacy for Nestlé brands. Far from undermining traditional channels (the big worry with brand-led DTC plays), the Nestlé Marktplatz—if managed well—will drive footfall and e-commerce traffic to those channels—via the advocacy effect produced by engaging customers as brand advisors.

One of the great advantages of social marketplaces is that buyers can share information about items that they intend to purchase or have already bought. The concept is like a collaborative swap meet: you sell and buy from people with the same style as you.

Also, unlike traditional online marketplaces such as eBay and Craigslist, where customers routinely transact with complete strangers, thus making them vulnerable to malicious cheaters out to defraud them, this reliance on friends or friends of friends leads to increased trust and along with it, improved customer satisfaction. And "trust" cannot be oversold, as consumers will likely not purchase products from merchants that they mistrust.

Marketplaces make good business sense from a social standpoint because they provide places where buyers and sellers can come together and monetize community content, and sellers can generate revenue from community interactions.

UNLOCKING SOCIAL SALES

The secret to unlocking social sales is to put buyers and sellers together in an online community where they have the freedom to interact on a personal level that fosters transparency and trust, and through which they can leverage their social graph and the influence of friends to make smarter buying decisions.

Here are several examples of companies that leverage both the commerce and social aspects of marketplace-style selling.

ETSY (WWW.ETSY.COM)

Etsy may be the mother of the social commerce marketplace movement. In fact, the site is on a mission to change the way the global economy works by providing very small businesses with the ability to sell handmade and vintage products to consumers in bazaar-style fashion.

From a commerce perspective, Etsy makes it possible for sellers to move from hobbyist status to full-fledged, full-time businesses. And, for buyers interested in hand-crafted or vintage items, it makes the job of product discovery much simpler. Socially, the site functions as an online community where buyers and sellers can come together to discuss the products they love.

PAYVMENT (WWW.PAYVMENT.COM)

With over 165,000 e-commerce merchants using its platform, Payvment is the largest shopping cart provider on Facebook. The success of the company doesn't lie merely with its shopping cart but with the fact that Payvment has curated the products offered by these merchants into a Facebook shopping mall. Buyers who visit the mall can find products based on multiple categories and interests of other Facebook users.

Through its emphasis on product discovery accompanied by its focus on leveraging the "interest graph" (see Chapter 15), Payvment helps customers shop smarter using their social intelligence.

AIRBNB (WWW.AIRBNB.COM)

AirBnB is a user-review-powered peer-to-peer market-place that allows people to share their homes with travellers around the globe.

The payoff for hosts is that it provides an added source of income, allowing them to monetize spaces they may not otherwise use. For renters, the many customer ratings, reviews, and testimonials build trust—and the fact that they can find lodging at all price points doesn't hurt either.

ENVATO (WWW.ENVATO.COM)

The Envato Marketplaces allow anyone to buy or sell digital goods like WordPress themes, background music, Adobe After Effects project files, Flash templates, and much more. The marketplaces are home to a community of over 500,000 users, authors, and buyers, and every day hundreds of new files are added. The site also provides a place where freelance designers can hive together to chat, share advice, and find jobs.

ADDOWAY (WWW.ADDOWAY.COM)

Addoway is similar to eBay in that it is a marketplace where anyone can buy and sell products. Unlike eBay, where sellers' identities are hidden behind usernames and access to them is primarily funnelled through the site itself, Addoway shows an avatar of the seller, along with links to social networks where he or she may have a profile. It puts the purchaser and the seller in direct communication.

OFFICE ARROW (WWW.OFFICEARROW.COM)

Office Arrow is a B2B social marketplace for office professionals. It represents a community of more than 5,000 sellers of office products and services. It's also a peer-to-peer network driven by customer ratings and reviews.

THREADFLIP (WWW.THREADFLIP.COM)

Threadflip is an Etsy-like social marketplace designed to let women sell the items they no longer wear, or share their own designs. Customers use credits to shop the closets of favorite designers, collectors, and friends, or cash out on products they have sold.

These sites solve a number of problems for shoppers. By bringing thousands of buyers and sellers together in one place, they enable product discovery on a grand scale, and do so in a social environment where shoppers can rely on the influence of friends to help them shop smarter. Because many focus on niche markets, they also foster social bonding ("birds of a feather") around shared interests.

Social marketplaces foster interaction between merchants and their customers. They facilitate customer reviews, feedback ratings, and shopping experiences. Consumers can tell the world whether they "Like" a merchant or a product. And merchants can share details of themselves, such as their names, faces, outside interests, and provide easy methods for consumers to communicate with them.

Interested in setting up your own social commerce marketplace? Here are some ideas to help you:

- Start by listing products on existing relevant marketplaces, whether in niche communities like Etsy or, depending on the range of products you offer, broader-based ones.

- To foster community, build social functionality into your e-commerce website; these could include peer-to-peer ratings and reviews systems, Facebook social plug-ins, blogs, forums, or groups. Tap into Facebook's Open Graph to further extend social connectivity and encourage social sharing.
- Global brands could follow Nestlé's lead and create a marketplace featuring products that might otherwise be available only in certain locales.
- Create Amazon-style marketplaces where you not only sell your own products, but allow others to sell, as well.
- "The riches are in the niches"; think Etsy or Office Arrow and establish niche communities around topics of interest to consumers.

SHOPPING FIRST, SOCIAL SECOND

Retail isn't broken. Stores are.

—Ron Johnson, CEO
JCPenney

SHOPKICK

Amie considers herself a pro-shopper. She's what's known in the trade as a "market maven"; she loves shopping and knows where to get all the best deals. Amie is the person her friends turn to when they want shopping advice. One morning, when she was trying on a new outfit in the fitting room at fashion retailer American Eagle, she noticed a poster on the door announcing, "Get rewarded for coming into the store and trying on clothes." Not only did it catch her attention, but it captured her imagination.

The poster was about a shopping app called Shopkick that rewards users just for coming into the store. Amie downloaded it then and there and was immediately rewarded with points—called "kicks" (as in kickbacks).

The Shopkick app and the rewards it provides made Amie want to shop more. In the few months since she first downloaded it, Amie has used the app dozens of times to collect points from stores like Best Buy, Macy's, Crate & Barrel, Target, and others, which she then uses for discounts on products, Facebook Credits, restaurant vouchers, iTunes gift cards, and more.

COMMERCE MINDSET

From a commerce mindset, business is ultimately all about solving your customers' problems (at a profit), and to the degree social media can be useful in solving customers' problems, it can be a useful business tool. And of course, the perennial customer problem is how to maximize value they get from spending their hard-earned cash. Shopkick helps solve the problem of these "value-maximizing" customers by getting them more, for less.

Therein lies the rub. Most retail stores have a misunderstanding as to why they exist. Stores are not merely places to pick up items housed on shelves or carried in an e-commerce catalog. Rather, they exist to solve shoppers' problems and make their lives better—through what they sell, how they sell it, and at what price.

But value is not all about price. "A store has got to be much more than a place to acquire merchandise. It's got to help people enrich their lives," said Ron Johnson, CEO of JCPenney.[1] And he should know. Prior to his current stint as the head of the venerable retail chain, Johnson served as VP of Retail for Apple, and is the man credited with the raging success of Apple Stores. In creating the concept, Johnson threw out the rule book and literally reinvented shopping from the ground up. As a result, Apple Stores became the highest performing stores in the history of retail.

In his view, this requires a shift away from a transaction mindset focused on selling more stuff to a value-creation mindset focused on *enhancing the shopping experience.* "[If] a store can help shoppers find outfits that make them feel better about themselves, for instance, or introduce them to a new device that can change the way they communicate, the store is adding value beyond simply providing merchandise," said Johnson.

Someone who shares Johnson's philosophy is Cyriac Roeding, cofounder and CEO of Shopkick, the app used by Amie that rewards customers just for coming into the store. Like Johnson, Roeding sees a need for a dramatic shift in the way consumers experience shopping in order to make it a more satisfying, even enjoyable, experience.

"If foot traffic is so important, then how come no one rewards you for coming to a store? No one has a clue you're there until you buy something with a credit card. They welcome you when you're leaving," said Roeding. "What we need to do is turn this around and welcome customers when they come in, not when they go out." His app is designed with that goal in mind.

A small box located in the store that emits a signal picked up by a smartphone mic is what sets Shopkick apart from other location-aware apps like foursquare. With the app turned on, the store literally "knows" you the moment you walk in and rewards you with points—"kicks"—just for entering. The more you interact with the store using the app, the more kicks you receive.

In their comments, both Johnson and Roeding hit on the secret to shopping, whether online or in physical stores, and that is *to add value to the shopping experience by going beyond just the transaction and giving them more than they expect.* Whether that expresses itself through a high degree of service, as is the case with Apple Stores, or through incentives such as reward points, if you make shoppers happy and put a smile on their face, you virtually guarantee they will return.

SOCIAL MINDSET

Solving shoppers' problems by adding value has a social dimension. The input, advice, and feedback from friends can add value to the shopping experience, as can the guidance of trusted experts.

However, utilizing social media to add value to the shopping experience requires a shift in mindset from "social first, shopping second" to one that puts shopping at the core with social as an added layer.

For instance, we go to social networks like Facebook not to shop, but to socialize. We may see a newsfeed item from a friend who has made a purchase, but that's incidental. Conversely, when we visit an e-commerce or social commerce site, it's usually with the intent to buy— shopping first, social second.

This fundamental misunderstanding about the proper role of social media is the reason retailers such Gap, GameStop, and JCPenney shuttered their Facebook stores in early 2012. Simply stated, they lacked any distinct value proposition. Instead, these stores were simply clones of existing e-commerce sites selling the same products for the same prices with the same promotions.

Without some unique value proposition to compel them, it is unreasonable to expect social networkers to equate social media with shopping. "Brands are not going to win by trying to move people from social to shopping," said Cyriac Roeding. "It feels awkward to start selling things in social environment. It has to do with intent."

Group-buy, local deal, and flash sales apps such as Groupon, Amazon Local, and Gilt foster this "shopping first, social second" intent. Consumers subscribe to these sites for the single purpose of getting a bargain, sometimes to the tune of 80 percent off the retail price. But it is the emphasis on shopping that, combined with the satisfaction of getting a good deal, stimulates social sharing. Again, shopping first, social second.

One other area where a mindset change is needed is in the perception that, somehow, shopping in the "real world" is different than in the online world. "In reality, what's growing is physical retailers' extension into a multichannel world. It's not as though there's a physical retail world and an online retail world, and as one grows, the other declines. They're increasingly integrated," said Ron Johnson.

Brick-and-mortar retailers especially need to embrace this idea of integration due to a relatively new trend called "showrooming," which is a practice where customers check out a product in the store, asking questions and examining an item, only to purchase it online, usually on a marketplace such as Amazon or eBay. In fact, you may already be using one of the popular "scan and scram" apps such as Amazon's "Price Checker" that allows users to scan a barcode then check the price for the same product on Amazon. While standing in the store aisle next to the actual merchandise, users can make the purchase online. Talk about adding insult to injury!

"Amazon is a significant threat to any retailer who doesn't understand the role of retail is fundamentally changing. As such, the biggest opportunity today is for retailers to utilize social technologies such as Shopkick to insert themselves where consumers are spending money, and that's through shopping," said Roeding. "This convergence of a digital layer on top of the physical can serve to benefit both retailers and shoppers through the added value it provides."

So where the social mindset is concerned, the secret to successful social commerce is to utilize social technologies to enhance the shopping experience, whether that happens on a retailer's e-commerce site or in the physical store.

UNLOCKING SOCIAL SALES

When properly aligned, social media provides a unique value proposition that can help solve shoppers' problems in terms of what to buy *and* provide the value-add needed to make the shopping experience more enjoyable. The following are some examples of brands that have implemented this concept:

- Part e-commerce site and part social network, **Bloom.com**'s mission is that women "never buy the wrong beauty products again." The site uses social technology to add shopper value by harnessing the wisdom and experience of thousands of women to provide an unbiased, trusted source for all things beauty. Users receive "Best4You" recommendations from other women who are considered to be beauty matches.

- In 2010, Italian fashion brand **Diesel** used a "Facebook Photo Mirror" that brought Facebook into the fitting room and allowed in-store shoppers to snap a photo of themselves trying on Diesel gear and post it directly to their Facebook profiles. Ostensibly the idea was to "friendsource" feedback and advice on what to buy in real-time.
- **Zappos** created an app called "TweetWall" that uses Twitter to let customers see what products people are talking about and which may be trending. Visitors can browse through the TweetWall image gallery and see product tweets as they are posted in real-time, then click through to make a purchase on Zappos' website.
- **American Express** card members can sync their eligible card with Twitter and when they tweet using special offer hashtags, couponless savings are loaded directly to their synced cards, which can be used either online or in-store at participating merchants.

Regardless of the techniques employed, smart merchants will ensure that the capability exists for shoppers to use their social intelligence and reliance on their network of friends to enhance the shopping experience. Here are some suggestions for how to go about it:

- Incorporate the use of Facebook's free social plug-ins on your e-commerce site to add a social dimension to the online shopping experience.
- Consider running check-in deals with foursquare, Shopkick, or Facebook to entice shoppers into the store and share their purchases.
- Think about integrating rating and review software so that customers can see what others like themselves think about a product.
- In-store, how about having a bestseller list displayed, or customer testimonials and reviews next to product displays.

- Online, use popularity lists to allow shoppers to view options by "most popular," "most viewed," and "most commented," which provide social proof as to what products are best to purchase.
- Utilize group-buy tools to allow shoppers to club together in order to get the best deal.

SELL TO NICHE MARKETS

The key to competing and surviving against Walmart is to focus your business into a niche or pocket where you can leverage your strengths.

—MICHAEL BERGDAHL, FORMER DIRECTOR OF "PEOPLE" WALMART

CRAFT BREWS

Jonathan has been a beer drinker since his college days. For years he's opted for mass-produced, mass-marketed brands that take up most of the shelf space in stores, like Budweiser, Miller, and Coors.

But since a friend introduced Jonathan to a craft beer online community called Pintley he's been rethinking his choices. On Pintley, he can read ratings and reviews posted by community members, learn from experts, share his own recommendations with friends and followers on Facebook and Twitter, and even dialogue with brewers themselves, who can use the site to promote their products via word of mouth. Some of the most well known are represented—brands like Samuel Adams, Harpoon Brewery, and Great Divide. More important, there are hundreds Jonathan had never heard of; niche brands that lack the marketing muscle and nationwide distribution of the big three.

Thanks to Pintley, Jonathan is turning into quite the beer aficionado, and everywhere he travels, instead of buying the most well-advertised brands, he looks for local microbrews that he can't find at home.

COMMERCE MINDSET

Though craft beers comprise only about 6 percent of the total beer market, they are quickly gaining in popularity in a market where beer sales of the big three producers are declining. The reason: whether based on locale (as many microbreweries are) or taste preferences, they have niche market appeal. They may not be widely loved, but they are *intensely* loved by those who favor them. And that leads us to our next secret: sell products that appeal to niche markets. Commercially speaking, niche selling can be more cost efficient and may stand a better chance of being effective, particularly in competitive markets.

The key idea that the future of commerce is selling *less of more*—by catering to multiple niches rather than pinning one's hopes on selling one or two blockbuster hit products—became popular, ironically, in 2006 with *Wired* magazine Chris Anderson's blockbuster bestseller *The Long Tail*. *The Long Tail* argued that sales in any product category follows a power curve: very few mass products sell a lot, while lots of niche products sell a little. Smart business today, the book argued, means selling to the "Long Tail" of multiple niches. In the Long Tail, competition is less fierce, risk is reduced, and there are multiple opportunities. And technology makes Long Tail selling viable: the Internet brings people with niche passions together and allows businesses to cater to them, while e-commerce and logistics technology have reduced inventory and selling costs enough to make selling to multiple niches economically viable.

While the validity of the Long Tail strategy has been hotly debated in various markets, the idea that niche selling is smart makes sense. Finding underserved markets that you can service better than anyone else is the key to unlocking sales.

No brand manufacturer has more mass marketing muscle than Procter & Gamble, but even this Goliath has found value in selling to niche markets. Take its laundry detergent line, for example. Arguably, P&G sells more laundry detergent than any other company on the planet; Tide, Gain, and Cheer are some of its premier brands.

Yet, in 2008, the company tested a version of Tide called Swash on an interesting niche market: college students who have a tendency to put off washing clothes. Swash was not a laundry detergent, but a line of products designed to freshen clothes between uses rather than washing them. The line included a spray to remove odors, a stain-erasing pen, a spray to remove wrinkles, and a moistened cloth that can be placed in a dryer to remove wrinkles.

Laundry detergent is not the only product category where Procter & Gamble has "found a niche." Personal care is another. In 2004, P&G marketed a line of products called OT Overtime—the name referred to the "overtime" period in sports—that were created exclusively for tween and teenage boys (ages 9–16). Not only that, the company's Head & Shoulders product line was developed based on a desire to target another niche: people with dry scalp and dandruff. And with its Crest Whitestrips product, P&G almost singlehandedly created a marketing niche, teeth whitening. It might not be overstating the case to suggest that many of its products were developed to have niche market appeal.

Gone are the days when average products made for average people held sway. Let's face it; people want choices. Visit any large grocery store and you're most likely to see multiple versions of everything from iced tea to toilet paper and even beer. It's the Long Tail in action. And, it's why companies like Zappos, Terracycle, Method, and Honest Tea have gained market share.

The adage goes, "You can please all the people some of the time, and some of the people all the time, but you can't please all the people all the time." When we're focused on reaching niche markets, we're opting to sell products that please only *some* of the people.

The truth is that everyone is not your customer. Therefore, it makes sense from a commerce mindset to appeal to only those who have a keen interest in your products and/or to sell products that target unfilled or partially filled niches.

SOCIAL MINDSET

Social media provides an ideal platform for companies to take a deep dive into niche markets. Consider Facebook, for example. With its ability to dissect markets down to even double digits based on user's "Likes" and interests, Facebook has become a niche-marketing nirvana. But the same can be said of Twitter, Pinterest, YouTube, and many other social networks or applications. Do a keyword search on any topic and there is a good chance you will find both content and conversations relative to it, so it's not difficult to imagine that brands could find receptive niche markets within them.

Craft brewery Great Divide partnered with Pintley[1] and used the site to encourage existing customers to share positive sentiment about the brand on Twitter and Facebook and to prompt new customers to buy and review its products.

In just over four weeks, the program produced more than 850 positive brand mentions on Twitter and Facebook, creating more than 223,000 potential exposures. Users wrote over 220 reviews and added Great Divide beers to their wish lists more than 2,500 times.

Best of all, the program produced significantly more results and greatly reduced costs compared to other, more traditional forms of marketing, like print advertising and trade shows. For Great Divide, marketing to an avid niche community of craft brew fans proved to be extremely advantageous, especially when combined with the viral syndication provided by social media.

Another interesting example is Orabrush, a product designed to freshen breath by cleansing the tongue. Despite thousands spent in advertising and sales pitches made to some brand-name pharmacies, as well as Colgate and OralB, the little known Utah-based company had failed to make a dent in the market.

Then Dr. Bob Wagstaff, the 75-year-old inventor of Orabrush, presented his challenge to marketing students at Brigham Young University. After conducting extensive research, most of the students came back and said that 92 percent of the target market would not buy his product. However, one student, Jeffrey Harmon, saw this challenge differently. Forget the 92 percent, he thought, and focus on the 8 percent who would. In his mind, that small percentage still represented millions of people. Dr. Wagstaff liked what he heard and hired Harmon to market the product.

The first thing Harmon did was get a few friends together, write a script, and recorded a kitschy video called "Bad Breath Test," which they launched on YouTube. The video went viral and product sales increased dramatically. That one video led to an entire series that have been seen by upward of 35 million viewers, making it the third most subscribed channel on YouTube, and over 1 million units have been sold.

Those videos, coupled with a $28 Facebook ad targeting Walmart employees at its headquarters in Bentonville, Arkansas, even led to a nationwide deal with the discount retailer.[2] Now, Orabrush can be found in 3,500 Walmart stores. But it all started with niche market penetration and social media got credit for the company's success.

In his seminal blog post, "1000 True Fans,"[3] *Wired* cofounder Kevin Kelly said that what brands should do is connect directly with "True Fans," which he defines as people who will purchase anything and everything you produce.

Even though he suggests that you only need 1,000 true fans (certainly 1,000 represents a niche market), whatever your number, direct connection with them is necessary, he says, in order to be successful. And he recommends social media as the avenue through which such connections can be made.

So, the secret to sales from a social perspective is to use social media to reach a niche market of people who will become fans and advocates of your brand.

UNLOCKING SOCIAL SALES

Niche market selling works from a commerce perspective because everyone is not your customer, so it makes sense to focus on reaching those who are. It makes sense from a social perspective because social media is an avenue through which they can be reached directly and through which content—blog posts, YouTube videos, Facebook status updates, product offers, etc.—can be easily shared.

So, how does this secret play out where social commerce is concerned? Use social commerce to build "social loyalty" among a niche community of true fans, those who have particular interest in what you have to sell.

There are a number of ways social commerce can be used to reach niche audiences.

GROUP-BUY

One way is through group-buy sites focused on narrow verticals. Sites like these range from beer, wine, and liquor to software to watches. Here are two such examples:

Poggled (www.poggled.com) is a Groupon-esque deal site for bars and clubs offering negotiated drink deals. What's interesting about Poggled is not how it works—it's the familiar Groupon-style formula where you subscribe to receive e-mail deal alerts (or follow the Poggled deal feed on Twitter or Facebook)—but the fact that, when you find a deal you like, you can register as a new member and purchase your chosen voucher to get VIP access and have the voucher redeemed at your chosen bar or club.

Similar to Poggled is daily deal site **Plum District**, which targets mothers and their families. The site offers deals on products like children's clothing and services like portrait photography.

FLASH SALES

Another way to leverage niche market social commerce is through flash sales. Gilt emphasizes several niche market sectors: fashion, home décor, food, and travel. Another is One Kings Lane, which focuses on home décor, and yet another is Vacationist, which specializes in travel and leisure.

ONLINE COMMUNITIES

Online community Fashism.com targets young, fashion-conscious teens and twenty-somethings who come together online to discuss style. Appealing to an entirely different niche, electronics retailer RadioShack has a community called RadioShackDIY that allows hobbyists to share their do-it-yourself projects with others. And the aforementioned Pintley brings craft beer enthusiasts together to discover, discuss, and recommend their favorite beverages.

SUBSCRIPTION CLUBS

Subscription-based e-commerce clubs, especially sampling boxes that help consumers discover new products, are popular ways to reach niche audiences. Blissmobox helps consumers discover delicious organic food, while BabbaBox helps parents discover educational toys for children. Birchbox sends monthly beauty product samples to women; Hiskit does something similar for men.

These sites and others like them solve customers' problems socially. Group-buy and flash sales sites allow consumers to club together to get steep discounts by buying in bulk. Vertically specific, interest-based communities and clubs create a sense of social bonding, where friends can rely on the opinions of others who share similar tastes to shop more intelligently.

The secret to unlocking social sales is to use social media to appeal to niche markets. Even though these may represent smaller percentages of consumers, going deep by tapping those with particular interests trumps mass marketing and can still mean access to millions of shoppers.

Here are some ideas to get you started:

- Run a Groupon-style group-buy site for a particular market niche; these can work in practically any product category or geographic locale.
- Market to ethnic groups who share similar subcultures, tastes, and desires; not only do ethnic products appeal to ethnic groups, but they also appeal to new "world" consumers looking to experience new products through consumption.
- Create a commerce-focused online community designed to appeal to specific interest groups; develop and leverage the community by sharing your passion and knowledge for whatever the niche is.
- If you're a technology vendor, rather than trying to sell to a variety of industries, dive deep into one or two vertical markets.
- Consider submitting your product line to flash sales sites and subscription clubs as a way to increase discovery and build loyalty.

GET RATED.
GET REVIEWED.

Your most unhappy customers are
your greatest source of learning.

—BILL GATES

ROTTEN TOMATOES

Jean doesn't trust advertising. She's been overpromised
and underdelivered dozens of times. Instead, she trusts
recommendations from friends and the opinions of others
like herself—fellow customers. This is why she refrains
from making a purchase without first reading what others have to say via online ratings and reviews.

Recently, she considered seeing the movie *The Hunger
Games* at her local theater. It had been heavily advertised

and highly touted, but Jean wanted to see what others who had already seen the film had to say, so she visited the movie review site Rotten Tomatoes.

Jean quickly parsed through reviews written by critics—after all, they are paid to write critical reviews—and immediately went to audience reviews. After reading a few reviews—there were almost a 1,000 pages worth—then making note of the overall rating of 84 percent the film received, Jean made the decision to see it. She was confident it would not be a disappointing waste of time and money.

For Jean, customer reviews on sites like Rotten Tomatoes, Amazon, and others provide valuable insights that help her make smarter purchase decisions. She benefits from the experience of others rather than her own.

COMMERCE MINDSET

Jean's example provides us with another secret to successful selling: encourage the use of customer ratings and reviews.

Prior to the advent of mass media and the advertising machine that accompanied it, people had no choice but to rely on word-of-mouth referrals from friends and neighbors before making purchase decisions. Even since advertising's coming of age, the use of and reliance on word of mouth regarding commerce decisions remains commonplace, and not without precedent.

According to Nielsen's latest Global Trust in Advertising and Brand Messages report,[1] which surveyed more than 28,000 Internet respondents in 56 countries, 92 percent of consumers around the world say they trust earned media, such as recommendations from friends and family, above all other forms of advertising.

Online consumer reviews are the second most trusted source of brand information and messaging, according to Nielsen, with 70 percent of global consumers surveyed online indicating they trust messages on this platform, an increase of 15 percent in four years.

This reliance on consumer reviews is even truer among Millennials, the generation born between 1980 and 2000. A study by social commerce platform provider Bazaarvoice[2] found that, while 66 percent of baby boomers turned to known parties for information and recommendations to influence their purchase decisions, most Millennials—51 percent—preferred anonymous user-generated content regarding buying decisions. That's a fact worthy of considerable attention, as Millennials will have more spending power than any other generation, according to Bazaarvoice.

Lastly, a study published by PowerReviews[3] showed that Internet users are taking more time to read reviews than in the past. 64 percent of shoppers spent ten minutes or more reading reviews in 2010 versus 50 percent in 2007. And 39 percent of customers read eight or more reviews before purchasing a product versus only 22 percent in 2007, said the study.

From a commerce perspective, there are any number of benefits to using consumer-driven ratings and reviews. They provide reassurance to the customer during the decision making process, relieving them of insecurities they may otherwise have. They also help customers find products that best fit their needs and guarantee a more satisfying shopping experience. For example, Toys 'R' Us has done a great job of aggregating user-generated content on its website to allow other customers to find items based on "fit" and "use."

Of course, the question has to be asked: do reviews written by consumers have a positive effect on sales?

A study by the University of Michigan's Ross School of Business,[4] which examined the relationship between the number of online reviews and sales, states conclusively that, indeed, it does. The study reports:

> Using data collected from a large online retailer
> of electronic products over a six-year period, the
> researchers found that the number of reviews has
> a significant positive effect on sales of products
> that are perceived favorably by consumers, while
> volume has a significant negative impact on sales
> of products with poor consumer ratings.

Marketing in the Groundswell, the book by Forrester Research analyst Josh Bernoff and former analyst Charlene Li, suggests that ratings and reviews allow you to "tap into customer's enthusiasm."[5] The authors cite Ebags.com, a company that, at the time the book was written, had experienced 30 percent annual growth year after year for the eight years it has been selling handbags and luggage online. The company "turned customers into a powerful asset" said the authors, and now places ratings and reviews front and center on its website.

Of course, there have been less than ethical uses of the rating and review practice. Some businesses fabricate reviews by anonymously posting only positive ones. Others filter out negative reviews. One company, VIP Deals, went so far as to include a note in orders for its Kindle Fire covers that said the company would rebate the purchase price in exchange for a positive review.

Despite such questionable tactics, customer testimonials, ratings, and reviews are still considered to be the most effective means of encouraging the degree of trust necessary to increase purchases. Therefore, from a commercial mindset, relying on the voice of the customer is paramount and a key to convincing prospective customers to buy.

SOCIAL MINDSET

Social media is unprecedented in its ability to provide average, everyday people with a voice to express opinions, critique products, and offer recommendations on those they like. Indeed, social media transports us back to a day when recommendations from friends trump every other form of advertising.

Further, social media can help overcome a consumer's reluctance to purchase products due to lack of trust. It fosters interaction between a brand and its customers, and easily facilitates customer reviews, feedback ratings, and shopping experiences. Plus, its viral nature means that those expressions can reach much further than in any other form of media.

Andy Chen, cofounder and CEO of ratings and review software company PowerReviews said, "Social media has flipped the original commerce model so that, now, it's bottom up. Customers take pride in purchase decisions and what they buy and aren't reluctant to share that information via social media."

From a purely retail perspective, perhaps no other company does ratings and reviews better than Amazon. Through its integration of features like star ratings, written reviews, and user profiles, Amazon made the use of such user-generated content a staple in the e-commerce world. If you do just one thing after reading this chapter, spend 5 minutes on Amazon and list all the ways that customer feedback is integrated into site copy. Then compare with your website.

Amazon distinguished itself in 2010 by integrating with Facebook to provide a new, more personalized layer of product recommendations. Users can view things like birthday and gift suggestions for friends, find out which items have been purchased and are popular among friends, and see recommendations on products from friends.

Consumer-driven ratings and reviews make sense from a social standpoint, thanks to its ability to help consumers make smarter purchase decisions due the reliance on the experiences of others, especially their friends, and its propensity to make consumer opinions easier to spread.

UNLOCKING SOCIAL SALES

Considering the benefits that consumer-driven ratings and reviews offer from both a commerce and social perspective—increased trust, viral reach, and the positive effect on sales—it makes sense for brands to combine the two. In doing so, social commerce becomes a force to be reckoned with.

Recognizing its massive potential, that's precisely what the big two rating and review platforms, now united as one company—Bazaarvoice and PowerReviews—have done. Both companies understand the value that the voice of the customer provides when it comes to how a brand is perceived.

Case in point, beauty brand Urban Decay, which incorporated the Bazaarvoice "Conversations" solution on its e-commerce website. In a case study on the brand,[6] Bazaarvoice reported, "Within seven months of Urban Decay's launch of Bazaarvoice Conversations, loyal 'UDers' had submitted over 27,000 product reviews with an average product rating of 4.8 out of 5." The report continues, "These reviews have had an overwhelmingly positive effect on conversion and revenue. Website visitors who interact with consumer opinions are 237 percent more likely to convert than those who don't. And the average revenue per visitor for these consumers is 230 percent higher."

To take full advantage of the social commerce proposition of helping people connect where they buy and buy where they connect, reviews were also integrated with Urban Decay's Facebook page, thus enabling customers to share them with their peers.

Building on its core competency of ratings and reviews, PowerReviews has two products that tie directly into Facebook: Facebook Discovery and Facebook Community. Using these products, consumers can choose to follow a reviewer, have future reviews published to their Facebook newsfeed, ask friends for advice on which product to buy by posting a question or poll to their Facebook wall, link their Facebook profile to reviews they've written, and engage with other reviewers by asking product-related questions.

In terms of ROI, PowerReviews estimates that each review from a company's website that is shared on Facebook is worth $15.72 in sales value. 57 percent of reviews written by Facebook members are shared to their newsfeed and 70 percent of all reviews shared to Facebook get a "Like" or a comment of some kind.

With that kind of evidence, is there any question that using ratings and reviews within a social commerce context will not benefit both brands and consumers? Since the answer is obvious, the next question is: how can you use consumer-driven ratings and reviews in innovative ways to sell more products? Here are some ideas for getting started:

- Look at how Amazon integrates customer feedback into site copy and product pages. Make a list and ask how you could do likewise.
- Incorporate Facebook's Open Graph to provide users with the ability to quickly share reviews on the social network after posting them on the brand's website; also allow users to import their Facebook profile information into the reviews they write.
- Make it easy to leave reviews on your website by employing the use of product review solutions such as those provided by PowerReviews, Bazaarvoice, and Reevoo.
- Don't filter or edit out negative reviews; having both positive and negative reviews builds trust and credibility.
- Incentivize customers to write reviews, but don't offer free goods (or cash) to customers in exchange for reviews.
- Ask fans and followers to submit reviews and include a link to the review from your website.
- Send a follow-up e-mail three weeks after a purchase requesting a review.
- Encourage customers to make videos of product reviews to post to YouTube; this works especially well when it comes to influencing the buying decisions of Millennials.

GO MOBILE

Put your best people on mobile.

—ERIC SCHMIDT, GOOGLE CEO

2001–11

STARBUCKS

Almost every day without fail, Madison heads to Starbucks to treat herself to another cup of her favorite elixir, a Grande Chai Tea Latte (usually accompanied by a blueberry scone).

When presented with the bill, Madison doesn't pay with cash or credit card. Instead, she pulls out her smartphone, launches Starbuck's mobile payment app, and presents it to the barista who scans the barcode showing on the screen, which dings her Starbucks Card for the amount owed. Easy.

For Madison, her smartphone is an essential. With it she can make purchases, check her bank balance, see what her Facebook friends are up to, text, tweet, Google, shop, play Words with Friends, and do a thousand-and-one other things all with a single tap. Oh, and she can make phone calls, too.

Madison lives in an untethered world where she is always on. She doesn't just use a mobile device; she lives a mobile lifestyle.

COMMERCE MINDSET

This brings us to our last secret for successful selling: embrace the use of mobile technology. *Go mobile.*

The growth of mobile technology is unprecedented. There are nearly 6 billion mobile subscribers—87 percent of the world's population. Of that number, over 1 billion are mobile web users. Mobile devices account for 8.5 percent of all global website hits, and many mobile web users are mobile-only. Of course, text messaging is still king of the mobile jungle, with over 8 trillion sent in 2011.[1]

What are mobile users doing with these hand-held miracle devices? What *aren't* they doing might be an easier question to answer. Mobile technology encompasses an entire ecosystem of use that includes gaming, search, music and entertainment, social networking, e-mail, texting, video, commerce, and more.

From a commerce standpoint, the growth of mobile technologies has many implications. For example, payments using mobile devices accounted for $240 billion in sales in 2011 and are expected to grow to more than

$1 trillion by 2015. $119 billion of that will come from e-commerce sales alone.

The Starbucks app alone accounted for 26 million mobile payments in 2011, a number that, by the end of March 2012, had risen to 42 million. Mobile app users are also tapping the company's e-gifting feature to send gift cards from their phones.[2]

Companies like Square and Paypal allow anyone with a checking account to take payments on their iPhone using a small device that plugs into the microphone jack. Google has turned phones into a mobile wallet where consumers can pay in-store simply by tapping their phones. Apple mobile devices, with their smart "Passbook" feature, store mobile passes, cards, and tickets from all kinds of services: movie tickets, boarding passes, loyalty and gift cards, and more. And because devices are location aware, the right ticket, card, or pass opens itself up as you get near the relevant store or location.

Why is this significant? Not because the tap is the real-world version of Amazon one-click and is more secure than chip-and–pin card payments, but because it has the potential to be a smart tap linking payments to contextual information (what's my account balance?), loyalty cards (reward balance?), coupons (how much did I save?), gift cards, receipts, boarding passes, tickets, and the list goes on.

In Chapter 17, we discussed the Shopkick app, which is revolutionizing in-store shopping by rewarding shoppers with points, called "kicks," just for entering the store. Big brands like Target, Macy's, American Eagle, Toys 'R' Us, and others are clamoring all over themselves to incorporate the app into their stores.

From an advertising standpoint, mobile growth is equally impressive. Ad clicks via mobile increased 711 percent in 2011, and ad revenue went up by 522 percent.[3]

However, retailers have a long way to go in terms of their adoption of mobile. For example, 51 percent of smartphone users say they are more likely to purchase from retailers with a mobile-specific website. Yet, fewer than 5 percent of retailers have one.[4]

The disruptive impact caused by mobile-enabled commerce has been so significant that, thanks in part to the "showrooming" (or "scan and scram") effect caused by shoppers using price comparison apps, Best Buy announced plans to close up to 50 of its stores in 2012. Sears announced that it would shutter as many as 120 of its stores, blaming mobile commerce as one culprit.

In a guest editorial at Forbes,[5] John Caron, senior vice president of marketing at Modiv Media, a mobile shopper marketing company, has some definite opinions about the growth of mobile commerce in 2012 and beyond. He sees this period as an era of "convergence and context."

Caron defines convergence as a time when "bricks and mobile finally integrate to provide a holistic shopping experience" within the confines of the physical store.

Context, he says, is when mobile "couponing, offers, location, check-ins, etc., become personalized to the individual shopper." It is the combination of those two trends that retailers need to understand in order to reinvigorate in-store shopping.

This is precisely what Shopkick is doing with its mobile application. It knows when you cross the store's threshold and provides the personalized experience that Caron prizes so highly he refers to it as "transformational."

Caron sees several benefits accruing from the incorporation of these trends among retailers, including saving shoppers both time and money, while providing a truly personalized, seamless shopping experience within the store.

According to Caron, the handwriting is on the wall. He says stores that embrace this methodology will thrive, while those who don't will continue to be "showrooms and warehouses for mobile apps that have displaced them."

Thanks to their mobile phones, consumers can get information to help with purchase decisions at the touch of a button, whether they are shopping online or in-store. What does this tell us? That, from a commerce standpoint, whether brick and mortar or online, it makes sense to invest in the use of mobile technology.

SOCIAL MINDSET

If the use of mobile technology has appeal from a commerce mindset, then it certainly does from a social mindset, for nowhere has mobile's impact been more significant than in social media. Take Facebook, for example. Its more than 450 million mobile users are twice as active as those who access the social network via a laptop or desktop computer, a fact that has not gone unnoticed by Facebook.

In 2011, Facebook opened its platform for use by mobile developers and, in 2012, rolled out its own app center designed, in part, to grow the number of mobile apps that use Facebook. In keeping with this, Facebook Credits can now be used as payment on mobile devices. So intent is Facebook on capturing mobile users, there is even talk the social network will launch its own smartphone!

The hegemony created by this coalescence of social and mobile is significant. In an article in the *Chicago Tribune*,[6] A. B. Mendez, senior research analyst at GreenCrest Capital Management LLC, said, "The combination of mobile and social is a potent one because mobility ups the amount of time consumers spend on the web, while social features increase interactivity with Internet content."

He stated, "A mobile and social web, both on the advertising side and e-commerce side, is going to be more highly monetizable." He added, "It's more likely to turn eyeballs and visitors into transactions and dollars spent."

Extending this social + mobile approach even further is the concept of the SOLOMO shopper. As mentioned in the Introduction, the term comes from the words social, local, and mobile, and was first used in 2011. It's a term that defines a new type of customer, one who combines the use of social media, mobile phones, and location-aware technologies to shop.

One of the early pioneers working with the SOLOMO concept is foursquare. While the service initially focused on letting friends "check in" to share information about their whereabouts via their smartphones, as the company grew to nearly 20 million users worldwide, with more than 2 billion check-ins, increasingly the company has turned its attention to local commerce. Foursquare built a self-service platform for merchants to offer deals that provide consumers with incentives to check in, including perks ranging from exclusive discounts, free merchandise, and even special parking spots.

Foursquare is not the only social network making use of a merchant-centered program. Facebook offers something similar with Deals. And, with its Groupon Now mobile app, group-buy deal purveyor Groupon has latched onto the SOLOMO concept. Using the app, consumers can find, purchase, redeem, and manage deals literally on the fly based on their interest and location. In fact, the company expects as much as 50 percent of its business will come from mobile in the next two years.

Other brands and retailers have taken the cue from four-square and are rolling out their own SOLOMO social commerce solutions. For instance, American Express' Link-Like-Love program sends mobile-friendly offers to cardholders based on their Facebook Likes and check-ins. In the UK, mobile operator O2 has launched it's own check-in rewards program.

More and more, mobile apps are being used to tap into existing social networks to create native communities and promote discovery, and web-based social networks are beginning to take advantage of mobile features and the accessibility they provide. Therefore, from a social mind-set, the use of mobile makes sense precisely because it provides users with the ability to interact with their social graph in real time, including at the point of purchase.

UNLOCKING SOCIAL SALES

Combine the benefits of mobile from a commerce mindset along with the ability to interact with information from friends and you have a compelling synthesis that, invariably, states it clearly: it makes sense to couple the use of mobile and social for commerce purposes.

People are using mobile devices to research, chat, book, share, blog, text, and tweet every aspect of the buying experience with their friends. Further, we rely on mobile at every point during the shopper journey—before, during, and after the purchase—to help us make smarter purchase decisions.

No one understands this transitional trend from traditional commerce (and e-commerce) to social commerce better than Marcus Whitney, CTO and cofounder of social commerce company Moontoast. He states, "The old web is basically broken for the way people consume it today. It doesn't respect the shift in power. Thanks to mobile technology, people have computers with them wherever they go, which gives them the ability to consume and post content wherever they are." He asserts, "The growth of mobile devices along with mobile payment capabilities is a significant trend in the disintermediation of commerce moving forward."

One company that not only embraces this shift, but was born from it, is Fashism.com, a site that brings together a community of young fashion-conscious consumers who gather around the ideal that "we" is better than "me," at least when it comes to making decisions about what to wear.

While sitting around a kitchen table one evening in 2008, Fashism founder Brooke Moreland and a few friends toyed with the idea of creating a site that addressed that need. Out of that informal meeting the die was struck for a website and mobile app that would allow members, using a smartphone, to take a picture of an outfit they were interested in purchasing, upload it to the site, and get instant feedback from members of the community.

Moreland's idea was born of her own shopping experience where she wanted to use mobile technology to garner the opinions of others about an outfit she was trying on, but couldn't because no such app existed at the time. So, she decided to build one.

In explaining her concept, Moreland said, "We built an online community incorporating both mobile and web-based technology where people post photos of themselves and ask the community whether they should buy or wear an outfit, then allow the community to discuss its merits."

When asked about the business model around Fashism, Moreland said, "We focused on utility first, with a view toward providing benefit to our users, believing that the money would come later. We didn't perceive it to be a problem as our members come to the site with a purchase intent."

Fashism does make money, however, via three channels: affiliate sales, advertising, and sponsored promotions with fashion brands. Moreland cited one example, a prom season promotion with Lord & Taylor. "Signs were posted in prom shop dressing rooms encouraging girls to post their photos to Fashism and claim their prom dress. Doing so gave them exclusive rights to the dress on our website," she stated. "If someone liked the dress, it would be pushed to the Lord & Taylor site where buyers could see dresses with similar attributes."

In summary, the use of mobile technology is growing by leaps and bounds, and mobile commerce is expected to grow commensurately. Add in the fact that social networking is one of the most predominant uses, and that people rely on the advice and influence of friends when making purchase decisions, and you are led to one conclusion: mobile-enabled social commerce is a trend that retailers must embrace, both now and in the future.

If any of this inspires you to delve more deeply into the use of mobile technology, here are some tips for how to start:

- As a basic first step, develop a mobile version of your website and e-commerce store; include Facebook login as a way to incorporate social media.
- Consider developing a mobile loyalty or payment app using Apple's Passbook or another service. Add social features such as sharing and gifting.
- Create a dedicated e-gifting app that allows customers to purchase gift cards for friends; combine a social component

that enables groups of people to club together to make the purchase.

- Don't fight the showrooming "scan and scram" trend; embrace it by helping mobile customers get the best deal . . . and share it with their friends.
- Consider a partnership with a third-party social commerce platform provider. Make sure you use one that has a mobile commerce component.
- Provide exclusive deals for mobile shoppers. Give reward points or extra discounts when they refer a friend.
- Use foursquare and Facebook Deals as a way to lure foot traffic and build loyalty.
- If you are a brick-and-mortar retailer, consider incorporating the use of mobile payment options such as NFS at POS terminals.
- If appropriate, investigate and consider the use of Facebook Credits as a method of payment.

Epilogue

A Chinese proverb says, "A journey of a thousand miles must begin with a single step." In *The Social Commerce Handbook*, we have attempted to provide 20 steps—principles—designed to help you begin your journey down the road to social commerce success.

These steps are not meant to be linear. Whether you choose to "play the impulse game," "sell with scarcity," "arm yourself with authority," "drive discovery," or "sell shovels," any one of these can be a first step. Doubtless, the journey will be different for each business putting these principles into action. The point is not "where" to begin, or even "how." The point is simply *to begin*.

We owe a debt of gratitude to social commerce pioneers who, often by trial and error, have paved the way for the rest of us to follow. So, too, do we owe our thanks to adventurous brands willing to experiment with the concepts and ideas outlined here.

Even though the journey has really just begun, a corner has been turned; social commerce is proving itself to have validity in the marketplace. Our goal with this book has been to provide some clear direction to help you avoid some of the detours and potholes you might otherwise encounter along the way.

With that in mind, it's useful one final time to reiterate some of the major themes contained in the book.

Social as a Service. Use social technology to help people shop smarter with their social intelligence by helping them solve problems socially—together. Additionally, help them to solve their social problems; specifically, how to bond with others and how to stand out from the crowd. A term used repeatedly throughout the book that best describes this mentality is "social utility." Hopefully, we have provided a sufficient number of examples to help you gain a clearer understanding of how to do this.

Re-imagine Shoppers. Change your thinking about the way people shop today. They use social media, location-aware, and mobile technologies to shop smarter. We call them the SOLOMO shoppers (social, local, and mobile). They are no longer on the horizon; they are in your stores, and they represent the future of shopping.

Put People First. If you take away only one thing from this book, let it be that social commerce is about *putting people first*. Social commerce is a very "human" approach to selling. It is about connecting with people, individually and collectively, based on their interests and shopping behaviors. It allows them to "drive the bus," and puts *their* needs, wants, and goals (rather than your own) foremost in mind.

At the outset of this book, we mentioned a question that's been asked by businesses and brands literally thousands of times: "How can I use social media to shift stock?" In response, let us ask one of our own: "Has that question been adequately answered?" We trust it has, and, if so, we challenge you to take the first step.

The poet John Ashbery said, "And so we turn the page over. To think of starting. This is all there is." You have reached the final page. It's now time to "turn the page over" and put into place the principles taught in this book. It has been our privilege to share them with you.

Paul Marsden and Paul Chaney

Notes

INTRODUCTION

1. The term "social media" appears to have been first coined by Darrell Berry back in 1995 in a discussion of "social media spaces"—the evolution of the web into a network of users rather than a network of pages; http://www.forbes.com/sites/jeffbercovici/2010/12/09/who-coined-social-media-web-pioneers-compete-for-credit.

2. See Bain's *The Ultimate Question 2.0* by Fred Reichheld and Bob Markey for these and other data points and insights into the power of customer recommendation.

3. Reported in *Social Commerce Today*; http://socialcommercetoday.com/how-to-calculate-fan-value-fan-economics-101.

4. Norman, L., *The Public Mirror: Molière and the Social Commerce of Depiction* (1999).

5. Reported in *Social Commerce Today*; http://socialcommercetoday.com/nike-social-commerce-pay-with-sweat-not-money-screenshots.

6. Reported in *Social Commerce Today*; http://socialcommercetoday.com/social-commerce-definition-word-cloud-definitive-definition-list.

7. For more on Bob Cialdini's insights, see Cialdini, R. B., *Influence: Science and Practice*, 5th ed. (Boston: Allyn & Bacon, 2009); *Influence: The Psychology of Persuasion*, Revised ed. (NewYork: Quill, Goldstein, 1993); Goldstein, N. J., Martin, S. J., and Cialdini, R. B., *Yes! 50 Scientifically Proven Ways to be Persuasive* (New York: Free Press, 2008). See also our original article in *Social Commerce Today*; http://socialcommercetoday.com/how-social-commerce-works-the-social-psychology-of-social-shopping.

8. Data from Marsden, P., *F-Commerce: Selling on Facebook* (2011) http://socialcommercetoday.com/documents/Syzygy_2011.pdf.

SECRET 1

1. Rook and Fischer, "Normative Influences on Impulsive Buying Behavior," *Journal of Consumer Research* (Dec. 1995): 305–313. (The Impulse Buying Scale is archived online at http://social commercetoday.com/how-to-sell-smart-on-facebook-insights-from -impulse-buying).

SECRET 2

1. Norton, M., "The IKEA Effect: When Labor Leads to Love," *Harvard Business Review* (Feb. 2009): 30.

SECRET 3

1. Tschohl, J., "Empowerment: The Key to Quality Service," *Managing Service Quality*, vol. 8, issue 6 (1998): 421–425.

SECRET 4

1. Kumar, V., Petersen, J. Andrew, and Leone, Robert P., "How Valuable Is Word of Mouth?" *Harvard Business Review*, 85 (10) (2007): 139–46.
2. Schmitt, P., Skiera, B., and Van den Bulte, C., "Referral Programs and Customer Value," *Journal of Marketing* 46, vol. 75 (Jan. 2011): 46–59.

SECRET 5

1. Cialdini, R. B., "Harnessing the Science of Persuasion," *Harvard Business Review* 79 (9) (Oct. 2001): 72–79.
2. Cialdini, R. B., *Influence: The Psychology of Persuasion.*

SECRET 6

1. Cialdini, R. B., *Influence: Science and Practice,* 4th ed. (Boston: Allyn & Bacon, 2001).

SECRET 7

1. Cialdini, R. B., *Influence: The Psychology of Persuasion.*

SECRET 8

1. Cialdini, R. B., "The science of persuasion," *Scientific American*, 284, (2001): 76–81.
2. Bazaarvoice, "Built by customers," *Whitepaper* (2011) http://bit.ly/yi4I7A.

SECRET 9

1. Milgram, S., "Behavioral Study of Obedience," *Journal of Abnormal Social Psychology* 67, (1963): 371–8.
2. Cialdini, R. B., "Harnessing the Science of Persuasion," *Harvard Business Review* 79 (9) (Oct. 2001): 72–79.

SECRET 10

1. McCarthy, M., "Bulls' Derrick Rose Inks $200 Million Shoe Deal with Adidas," *USA Today* (Feb. 26, 2012).
2. Elberse, A., and Verleun, J., "The Economic Value of Celebrity Endorsements," *Journal of Advertising Research* (forthcoming).

SECRET 11

1. http://brandgenetics.com/purple-cow-speed-summary.
2. "Why Discovery Must Evolve to Save Social Commerce," *Forbes*, Dec. 2011; http://www.forbes.com/sites/ciocentral/2011/12/19/why-discovery-must-evolve-to-save-social-commerce.

SECRET 12

1. Kawasaki, Guy, *The Art of the Start: The Time-Tested, Battle-Hardened Guide for Anyone Starting Anything* (New York: Portfolio, 2004).
2. Warren, Rick, *The Purpose Driven Life* (Grand Rapids, Michigan: Zondervan, 2002).
3. Carnegie, Dale, *How to Win Friends and Influence People*, Revised Ed., (New York: Simon & Schuster, 1981).
4. Olsen, Kate and Livingston, Geoff, "Cause Marketing Through Social Media: 5 Steps to Successful Online Campaigns," *Network for*

Good;   http://www1.networkforgood.org/ckfinder/userfiles/files/
CauseMarketingThroughSocialMedia.pdf.

5. "2010 Cone Cause Evolution Study," *Cone Communications*, 2010;
http://www.coneinc.com/files/2010-Cone-Cause-Evolution-Study
.pdf.

SECRET 13

1. Lecinski, Jim, "ZMOT: Winning the Zero Moment of Truth," April
2011, Google.

2. "Social Impact Study 2012 Infographic on Social Sharing," March 29,
2012, SociableLabs.com.

SECRET 14

1. http://hbr.org/2012/03/bad-reviews-can-boost-sales-heres-why/
ar/1.

SECRET 15

1. Scott, David Meerman and Halligan, Brian, *Marketing Lessons from
the Grateful Dead: What Every Business Can Learn from the Most Iconic
Band in History* (New York: John Wiley & Sons, 2010), 70.

2. "So What Comes After Social Commerce?," GigaOm, April 19, 2011;
http://gigaom.com/2011/04/19/so-what-comes-after-social
-commerce.

SECRET 16

1. http://laurelpapworth.com/etsy-com-online-community-revenue.

2. "Agora," Wikipedia; http://en.wikipedia.org/wiki/Agora.

3. "Samuel Brannan," Wikipedia; http://en.wikipedia.org/wiki/Samuel
_Brannan.

SECRET 17

1. "Retail Isn't Broken, Stores Are," *Harvard Business Review*, (Dec.
2011).

SECRET 18

1. "The Pintley Difference: A Marketing Case Study with Great Divide Brewing," February 2011; http://www.pintley.com/downloads/casestudies/Pintley_GD_CaseStudy.pdf.
2. "How Social Media Landed Orabrush a Walmart Deal," SS|PR, November 16, 2011; http://sspr.com/social-media-pr/case-study -social-media-landed-orabrush-walmart-deal.
3. Kelly, Kevin, "1,000 True Fans," *The Techium*, March 2008; http://kk.org/thetechnium/archives/2008/03/1000_true_fans.php.

SECRET 19

1. "Global Trust in Advertising and Brand Messages," *Nielsen*, April 2012; http://blog.nielsen.com/nielsenwire/media_entertainment/consumer-trust-in-online-social-and-mobile-advertising-grows.
2. "Millennials Look to Digital Word-of-Mouth to Drive Purchase Process," *eMarketer*, February 2, 2012; http://www.emarketer.com/Article.aspx?id=1008810&R=1008810.
3. "5 Social Shopping Trends," *PowerReviews*, May 26, 2010; http://www.powerreviews.com/assets/new/research/powerreviews_research_5socialtrends.pdf.
4. Etzion, Hila, "Examining the Relationship Between Number of Online Reviews and Sales: Is More Necessarily Better?," University of Michigan Ross School of Business, July 18, 2007.
5. Li, Charlene, and Bernoff, Josh, "Marketing in the Groundswell," Harvard Business School Press, June 18, 2009: 92.
6. "Conversations Lead to Conversion for Urban Decay," *Bazaarvoice*, May 9, 2012; http://www.bazaarvoice.com/resources/case-studies/conversations-lead-conversion-urban-decay.

SECRET 20

1. "Global Mobile Statistics 2012," MobiThinking, February 2012; http://mobithinking.com/mobile-marketing-tools/latest-mobile -stats.

2. "Starbucks Apps Account for 26M Mobile Payments and $110M in Card Reloads," *Venturebeat*, December 5, 2011; http://venturebeat .com/2011/12/05/starbucks-mobile-pay-stats.

3. "Infographic: One Year—700% Mobile Growth," *MarketingTech blog*, February 2012; http://www.marketingtechblog.com/mobile -ad-ctr-infographic.

4. "Social Commerce and the Smart SoLoMo Consumer," *Social Commerce Today*; July 5, 2011; http://socialcommercetoday.com/ social-commerce-the-smart-solomo-consumer-infographics.

5. Caron, John, "For Mobile Commerce: The Year of Convergence and Context," *Forbes*, January 16, 2012; http://www.forbes.com/ sites/ciocentral/2012/01/16/for-mobile-commerce-the-year-of -convergence-and-context.

6. "Internet Firms Grow on Concept of Copy and Conquer," *Chicago Tribune*, March 16, 2011; http://articles.chicagotribune.com/2011 -05-16/business/ct-biz-0516-social-commerce-20110516_1_mobile -application-local-commerce-internet.

Index

Note: Boldface page numbers indicate illustrations.

About the Authors

Paul Marsden, PhD, is a consumer psychologist specializing in digital technology, brand communication, and shopper marketing. With a PhD in social psychology, Paul launched Brainjuicer.com, now a leading online consumer research agency with a market capitalization of over $50 million. *Research Magazine* calls him "The Thought Leader" and has voted Paul a Top 50 Researcher. He now works with consumer brands and their agencies, helping them understand emerging market opportunities and develop effective brand strategies for the digital age. Former managing editor of the *Journal of Memetics*, he runs *Social Commerce Today*, the leading online publication for news, comment, and analysis on how to sell with social media. He is a contributor to the *New Scientist* and *The Psychologist*, and a member of the Royal Society of Arts.

Paul Chaney, known to many as "The Social Media Handyman," is a social media, social commerce, and Internet marketing consultant, popular speaker, trainer, and author of three books, which included *The F-Commerce Handbook* and the *Realty Blogging*. Paul provides Internet marketing consulting and training services to small and medium businesses, advertising agencies, and nonprofit organizations. His expertise lies in effectively combining the conversational marketing aspects of social media with conversion mechanisms that are fully aligned with business objectives. Paul sits on the board of advisors for the Women's Wisdom Network, the Social Media Marketing

Institute and SmartBrief on Social Media. He is a feature writer for *Practical Ecommerce* on the topic of social commerce and is associate editor of *Social Commerce Today*, a leading blog covering the topic of social commerce. He is a sought after speaker on the topic of social media marketing and has led numerous social media workshops throughout the United States and abroad. He was invited by the U.S. Department of Commerce to lead a series of social media workshops for businesspeople in the Ukraine.